# The Wedding Bible

BY

## Kate Harvey

# All you need to know to get hitched!

## Kate Harvey

# Dedication

To my bestest girls, my original wedding helpers, Bethany and Holly

I love you more x

# Introduction.

The "how to" guide into getting married.

This little guide gives you an insight and outline of my 20+ years of wedding experience and all the knowledge I have collated in that time. It gives you the background into the wedding industry and all the important things you need to know, do, and plan, as well as all the ins and outs of weddings and getting hitched in this day and age. I will give you an insight into the old wedding traditions set in a new world. Moreover, I will share information, advice, thoughts, and ideas to help you along your merry little way.

Write your own notes, ideas, and keep-sakes in the spaces provided after each section.

So without further ado, may I just take this opportunity to say congratulations on your engagement and happy planning? Are you ready? Let's start planning.

# Contents

# Where to start

So you're engaged, living together, and taking the plunge into creating your happily ever after. But where do you start in the planning process for your dream wedding?

First things first, choose the ideal time of the year you would like to get married. Whether it's a winter wonderland, springing into new beginnings, or any other time, what will make you both happy? What kind of look do you want to achieve? Do you need it to be in the school holidays or not? These questions will help you determine what time of the year you would prefer to get wed in. Once you have that, are you tied to dates? Do you want a particular date? Does a particular number mean something to you both?

Struggling? Then have a look at the dates and seasons part in this book; it may give you some inspiration and food for thought.

If you got the above, then all you need is the year you want to get married. Are you taking your time, saving, and planning? Or is it a case of no time like the present?

Well done, your first step is accomplished!

As trivial as it is to think about money and budgeting, this is your next step to decide how much you can afford to spend on your wedding and how much you need to save and budget. This also may determine the year you get married.

Working this out is no easy feat. It's not every day you plan a wedding, and it's hard to plan for unexpected costs that crop up, but if you put the time and effort into this now, it will hopefully ensure you'll live happily ever after wedding-debt free.

So let me break it down for you.

### Counting your cash

Do you and your partner have any savings at the moment? Leaving aside your in case of emergency funds, how much does that leave you with? Could any of that be put towards your wedding fund?

Can you set aside any wedding fund money from your current income and your partners? Once you have paid your existing debts and put your house/bill money to one side, can any of this be added to your wedding fund?

Ask your parents or loved ones if they would be willing to contribute to your wedding fund; don't assume they will automatically do it. It's nice to be asked.

### If you spend it, note it

Creating some sort of spreadsheet or list of spending will help you along the way. For example, it will help you see where you need to reign it in a bit or spend a bit more in other areas. List your estimated spending in one column and your actual spending in another.

When you're going and seeing venues, churches, venue stylists, dress shops, etc., all these need to go in your estimated list until you've decided who to go with or what to buy.

Make sure you ask vendors if the VAT is included in their costs, as you don't want that to be a surprise later on.

Also note, if you're planning your wedding for so many years to come, don't forget to ask if the price still stands at what it is today or if it will a % go on top of the price you have discussed. If so, ask how much that will be so you are not surprised with a new figure that you've not accounted for later on.

## Prepare yourself for surprises

Before you sign any contracts, read the fine print.

Check to see what is actually covered in their contract and see if their setup and breakdown fees are included in their cost. Make sure the contract matches what you've discussed and that the contract has all been adjusted and is relevant to your wedding, needs, and wants.

Don't sign it if it needs tweaking, get it changed, and don't presume it will all be okay, as it's what you've discussed; a verbal agreement isn't as concrete as a written one.

## Getting all the credit

However tempting it is to boost your cash flow with credit cards, don't go overboard. You'll get stuck with interest payments if you can't pay it off 30 days later.

If you do use them, try choosing one with a cash-back incentive or 0% interest payment plan.

## Savvy saving tips

Over budget?

Consider these ideas to curb your spending and save a few pounds.

- Change the venue. Before you commit to your venue, maybe see if there is more out there that you like that includes more in their package to save you money!
- Edit and re-edit your guest list. Be ruthless when you consider the extras you buy/make for each guest. It is a lot more than just your venue's price per head.
- Consider off-peak times. There will be a price difference with certain vendors. Summer months, weekend days, and school holidays are all more expensive.
- Hosting the ceremony and the reception in the same place will save you on transport costs.
- Do you need the live band, or will a DJ cut it?
- Can you DIY any of your arrangements in advance yourself?
- Say no to any upgrades you don't feel are right for your day.
- Check what else your vendor can provide. They may make an offer if you hire more than 1 item from themselves, they may have package deals, and it's worth an ask if it's money back in your pocket.

**Notes.**

# Legal jargon

Calling all over 16-year-olds, single, widowed, divorced, and free from a civil partnership people. Is that you? Then you are free to wed.

**Marriages can take place in:**

- A registry office
- Approved by the local authority premises (for example, a hotel)
- Outdoor licensed venues
- Church of England or a Church in Wales
- Synagogue or private place if both partners are Jewish
- Registered religious building in England or Wales
- In the home of one of the partners, if the partner is housebound or in prison
- In the hospital, if one partner is seriously ill
- Licensed naval, military, or Air Force chapel

**Legal requirements that must be met in order to marry:**

- It must be conducted by an authorised person to do so or by someone in the presence of an authorised person, and they must be registered to do it in that district.

- It must be entered into the marriage register, signed by both of you, 2 witnesses, the person who conducted the ceremony and/or the person authorised to register marriages.

- You must give notice at the registry office of your intended marriage, even if you are not marrying in that district. If you don't live together and your partner lives in another district, you will have to give notice to both registry offices. You will then be issued with authority to marry.

- You must give the registry office 28 days' notice before you can get hitched in England and Wales, and you must get hitched within 12 months of giving that notice. Both of you must be a resident for 7 days before the notice is given, and you must also state where the marriage is to take place in your notice. This is also not free, and you will have to pay to do this.

- During the time of giving your notice and ceremony, anyone wanting to object to your marriage can do so. But they would have to have strong grounds to do so, as it is a criminal offence if it turns out to be a false accusation.

**Remarriage:**

- If you are widowed, divorced, or in a civil partnership, and it has been dissolved. Nothing is stopping you from marrying again in a civil ceremony.

- Suppose you want to remarry in a religious ceremony. In that case, you will need to check with an official of that relevant religion, as they all have different rules about people remarrying in a religious setting, unfortunately.

## Marriage visas:

- If you are not a British or Irish citizen.
- You do not have indefinite leave to remain in the UK.
- You do not have pre-settled/settled status or have not applied for this before 30/06/2021.
- You are travelling to the UK to marry a British citizen, EEA, or someone settled in the UK.
- You are a non-EEA national, and you do not want to live in the UK.
- You will need to apply for a marriage visa or permit to get married or form a civil partnership here in the UK.
- The visa or permit you need will depend on where you or your partner are from and where you want to live in the UK after your ceremony.
- Please contact your local authority or the home office for the correct visa application you need to get married legally.
- Everyone wishing to marry will need to provide proof of their nationality.
- Any marriage cannot occur until all the necessary residency qualifications are met. This applies if one partner is living outside of the UK.
- All procedures must be adhered to if the marriage takes place in England or Wales and one partner lives in Scotland or Northern Ireland.

**Pre Nups:**

- If you want to guard your millions, assets, properties, and any other riches, a pre-nuptial agreement is a contract you need to get signed should the unfortunate thing happen and you divorce.
- This can be legally binding, and it could be good to have it in place so you can outline how you both wish to divide money and property, etc., should the unfortunate happen.
- Seek specialist advice from a solicitor before you enter into an agreement.

**Notes:**

# Church/Civil/Destination weddings

Let's start with the good ol' traditional church wedding. Here's what you need to know.

- Unless your partner is a non-EEA national, the Church of England and the Church of Wales are allowed to register your marriage at the same time as performing the ceremony.
- For all other religious marriages, you will need to give 28 days' notice of your marriage to the registry office.
- All ministers, priests, and other religious figures must have a certificate or license and be authorised to register marriages.
- In other religions, if the official person performing your ceremony is not authorised, a registrar must attend your religious ceremony to complete the official register for your marriage.
- If you want to get married outside of England and Wales, you must follow the procedures of that country's law.
- It is a legal requirement that your banns be read out in the parish where each of you lives, as well as the church in which you are to be married if it's somewhere else. These must be done for 3 Sundays during the 3 months before your wedding.

**Church fees:**

- The basic fee, approximately £560, depends on whether you get married in your parish. The basic fee will include the cost of the vicar, the church itself, the calling of your banns, a banns certificate, lighting, and all paperwork apart from your marriage certificate.

- Your marriage certificate, once registered at your registry office, can be paid for and collected there. This is approximately £11 per certificate.

**Extra fees for the church:**

These are your choice if you choose to have them for your wedding.

- Support of a verger helps with the church's cleanliness and tidiness. Can assist with handing out orders of service, hymn books, etc.
- If you want an organist to play your wedding music for the ceremony or the choir to sing your hymns, etc., these people are an additional fee.
- *The bells, the bells* (Disney's hunchback of Notre Dame movie quote). If you want the bells to chime and announce your wedding, this too, is extra.

**FYI**: if you choose to have your wedding filmed in the church, the musicians can request an increase in their fees for professional performing rights!

Also, some churches have local flower arrangers that go in and do the church flowers, so you may want to find out what floral arrangements they are. Can any additional flowers be arranged in the church by your florist? Some churches are sticklers for using any other supplier in their church, so it's best to check what you can and cannot do. Also, check what colours the arrangements come in, as they may clash with your colour scheme.

**Tips/Guidelines/Expectations for church marriages:**

- Meet with the priest/pastor/vicar/reverend or any other clergy member, ask them questions, this is your opportunity to feel out the location, feel which church you are most connected to, figure out the rules and regulations of the church, take notes and see if it fits in with you guys.

- Don't forget to ask about the church's event calendar, especially if you want to get married around a specific holiday period. They may already be fully booked. But also with this, they may have additional decor or special decorations that you may be able to utilise for your wedding, saving you some pennies.

- Music! Traditional churches may have limitations on what music you can play. Ask what you are allowed to do before you sign away.

- Photographers may need to abide by certain rules within the church. They may not be able to use flash photography. Again ask what's allowed within the church so no potential problems arise, especially on your big day. Some churches may not allow videographers, too. You will have to check with the church before signing up for one of these suppliers.

- Does the church have a dress code? Should shoulders be covered up, for instance? What is the general guideline for your guests?

- Do you both have to be of the same religion to get married in your chosen church? Some churches may enforce converting to the religion, so you are both the same. Best to check, guys.

**Documents your church may need to see include the following;**

Proof of baptism/confirmation or communion.

Marriage annulment.

Passport or birth certificate.

**FYI**, premarital counselling or pre-cana may be required. This is usually undertaken during a workshop at the church over a weekend or several weeks. Each church is different, and some churches do not require this at all.


**Things to discuss with your clergyman;**

- You may need 3 hymns you would like for your service.
- Walking down the aisle music, signing the register music, and leaving the church music.
- Which Bible readings would you like?
- Any readings/poems/special requests/prayers you would like to include?
- For wedding rehearsals, make sure you know when they are and attend them, so you don't fluff up your lines or forget how you are walking into church. Maybe include your bridal party so they don't feel the pressure on the big day itself. Maybe introduce your photographer when you have booked them so they can get a feel for the place and be inspired.
- Is there a contemporary wording choice for vows that can be used instead of the traditional wording? Is there an adaptation for the giving away part of the service? There may just well be a modern version or a traditional version for you to choose from.
- Does your church hold a Church Copyright Licence from CCLI? If they do, your church can record the wedding ceremony.

**A typical order of service at church:**

- Family and friends gather at the church, and they are seated, and partners wait in anticipation at the altar.
- Entrance of the bride
- Welcome and introduction by the clergyman
- Hymn
- Readings
- Sermon
- Exchange of Marriage Vows
- Prayers
- Hymn
- The signing of the register
- The final blessing
- The big smooch
- Exit

**Notes:**

# Civil ceremonies

Civil ceremonies are still legal ceremonies, just not religious; you cannot include anything from the Bible or the Torah.

They may suit your own personal tastes better.

**Things still included in a civil ceremony:**

- Legal registrar to conduct the ceremony
- The signing of the register
- Traditional/Modern vows
- Include readings, songs, and music
- Marriage certificate
- You still get to walk down the aisle and do everything you would in a church, just no religious chatter.

**Traditional civil ceremony vow:**

*Exchanging of the rings*

"I give you this ring as a symbol of our love. All that I am, I give to you. All that I have I share with you. I promise to love you, to be faithful and loyal, in good times and in bad."

**Where can civil ceremonies be held:**

- Registry office
- Town Hall

- Hotel
- Banqueting halls
- Restaurants
- Stately homes
- Approved place by the local authority

**Civil ceremony fees:**

Whether you get married in a stately home or a hotel, your basic registrar fees will still need to be paid in addition to your choice of venue and the costs to hold your wedding at their place. You will need to phone and get in touch with your local registry office to book their requirements when you have chosen your venue etc.

The basic registry office fees you will have to pay are:

- The administration ceremony booking fee is usually around £30
- Notice of marriage is approximately £35 per person. This has to be paid at the time of booking
- Registrar's fees will depend on the following:
    a) What time you get married
    b) What day you get married on
    c) If you are getting married in the registry office or at an alternative venue
    d) What district are you getting married in
    e) How many people are at your ceremony as you may need 2 registrars
    f) If your venue is an approved venue

All these arrangements decipher your registrar fees.

- Marriage certificate £11 each

So wherever you get married, you must book all your counterparts at the registry office, separate from your chosen wedding venue.

**FYI:**

Just a bit of civil ceremony knowledge for you:

- You do not have to live in the same district where you want your marriage to occur, but you do have to give notice to the registry office in that district of your marriage.
- Before you give formal notice to the registry office, you must have got your chosen wedding venue down to choices A and B.
- Once you have given your formal notice to the registry office, you have to wait 28 days before you can get wed, and if you are a non-British national, you will have to wait much longer.
- Once you have given notice, you have a year to get hitched!

Enjoy venue shopping!

**Notes:**

# Destination weddings

Sun, sea, sand, stress?

Getting married abroad might seem like a bit of a headache. Still, many tour operators now include local wedding planners in their costs, which will help you have a stress-free wedding abroad. However, if you're feeling brave to take on the task yourself, do your research and ensure you have all the right documentation, and you're onto a winner. So let me help you with it.

## Where to?

This is probably your first hurdle, so why not do this little task between yourselves, write a list of the key things you would like to have included, such as countryside, views, beach, etc. Is there a certain country you see yourself getting married in? Think of your ideal location. Then you can narrow down the destinations by your budget and the budget of your guests. Here are some of the most popular countries to get married in;

- Italy
- United States
- Cyprus
- Greece
- France
- Denmark

If you are smart with your destination, it may not cost you as much financially. Maybe choose a place with lots of all-inclusive resorts.

Sometimes the hotels fight over each other who has the affordable packages, and you might be able to use that to your advantage.

Maybe choose a less well-known city in a popular country.

Overall the destination should suit your personalities.

**Essential documents you'll need:**

You may need to contact the local authorities of where you want to get married to find out for sure what documents you need, but here are the basics:

- Full passport with at least 6 months left before it expires
- Full birth certificates
- Decree absolute if either of you is divorced
- Death certificate of spouse if either of you is widowed (and that marriage certificate)
- Deed poll proof of name change if you've changed your name
- Certificate of no impediment (CNI) from HMRC so you can legally get married abroad
- Adoption certificate if you're adopted
- Single-status statutory declaration (for people who have never been married)
- Medical test

They will need to be the originals or certified copies. Depending on the country you get married in, many of the above may need to be notarised before use. Some may need an apostille stamp or further legalisation. Some countries may also need you to translate the documents into the language of the country you want to wed in.

Take photocopies of all documents for yourself and your peace of mind and take them with you just in case.

Your marriage needs to meet the legal requirements of both the country you want to get married in and the country you live in.

If you are doing this yourself and not through a wedding planner, please ensure you have all the right legal documentation and that it gets to the right people in time for your wedding to be legal.

If you do use a wedding planner, all the documentation costs should be in their quote, so watch out if you start getting lots of hidden costs along the way.

## The legality of getting married abroad:

Many countries have a minimum time to stay in the country before you can obtain a marriage license. Check with the local authority or your wedding planner what this is.

Do your research. Some countries have other specific requirements you need to get before your marriage license. For instance, in Mexico, you need to have a blood test in a Mexican hospital before you wed.

Before you leave the UK, check with the local authority of the country you're marrying in that all your bases have been covered.

You must be old enough to get married in the UK and the country you're marrying in.

Is what you're doing allowed under UK law?

Check if you need a visa to visit the country you're marrying in. You can do this on the HMRC website.

## FYI:

Whatever path you go down to get married abroad, whether through a tour operator or you are going at it alone, here are a few titbits that you may not have thought of but still need to do.

- Take out wedding insurance as well as your travel insurance. Your travel insurance will not cover the potential problems arising from a wedding abroad.

- Your wedding insurance won't cover you for your honeymoon, so make sure your travel insurance does.

- Speak to your airline in advance concerning your dress. Although some might let you take it as hand luggage, you can actually buy specific hand luggage boxes for this purpose.

- Talk to your dress designer too about packing or folding your dress in a way to decrease fold and crease marks.

- Take pictures on your phone of makeup styles and hairstyles you like so you can show the stylists your vision and the ideal look you're going for. You may need a translator if they don't speak English.

- Get your quotes broken down in writing so you know what's expected and what isn't so that you can budget easier.

- You're getting married abroad for a reason, embrace the culture, and maybe let it influence the ceremony, the food, or the wine.

- Don't forget about your guests. Check to see if the flights are reasonable, and maybe create a wedding group to drop links in for websites, flights, accommodation, etc. Make sure you give them enough notice so they can plan, too, take time off work, apply for a visa if necessary, etc.

- Check, check and check again that your details are all booked in the right name and match your passport. And don't book your return flight in your new married name unless you've changed it by deed poll.

- Trust in yourself, and trust your wedding planner. Ask the questions, and get clarification but always check the required documentation yourself if you're using a wedding planner, just in case, as we are all human.

**Don't forget your passport!**

**Booked it, packed it.**

**Notes;**

# Venue's/Outdoor weddings;

Got your budget in mind? Let's go venue shopping, but where do I start, I hear you say?

Here is what to look for in choosing your venue:

## Location, location, location

- Do you dream of a lakeside wedding, city chic in a luxury hotel, rustic charm in the countryside, or a tipi in a field?
- Your venue and its location need to match your personalities
- Have you asked yourself what the ideal location for you both is?
- Will the location of your venue influence who attends your wedding?
- Will your guests have to travel?
- Does your venue need to be easily accessible for any disabled guests?

Why not have a few days trips out, go and view some of your venues, and get a feel for things? Seeing something in person will give you real clarity, and you might even surprise yourself with your findings.

## Capacity and availability;

Another important factor to consider is the size of the venue for the size of your guest list.

- What are your guest numbers?

- Does this impede your choice of venue?
- Are there alternative rooms? Maybe you're having a more intimate ceremony and don't need the oversized room, or maybe you've got hundreds wanting to attend, and you need the ballroom, make sure you ask the questions, so it suits your day and your requirements.

**Checking to see what dates are available, maybe consider:**

- Do you need to get married on the weekend? As it may be cheaper to get married during the week.
- Do you need to get married in the summer? As it may be cheaper to get married in the winter.
- Do they have any late availability or less expensive rates, say on the 13th of the month or Halloween?
- Are your dates around specific holidays, such as Christmas or Mother's Day? Will this impede on their price and availability for your wedding?

With the ideas you have in mind for your wedding and the overall theme you want to achieve,

does the venue cover this?

Is the room or space provided big enough?

Does it check off a few of your requirements?

These are some of the questions you need to ask yourself to see if the venue is right for you.

**Outdoorsy?**

If you have an outdoor wedding, here are some of the things you may need to check to see if it's still right for you:

- Is the land big enough to cover the tipi or marquee?
- Is it easily accessible?
- Is there enough space for toilets?
- What about food trucks, drink and dessert trucks, or any other catering supplies? Is there room on-site?
- Do you need space for outdoor games?
- Where can you stay the night of your wedding?
- Will you need to put on transport for guests to and from the site?
- Can guests stay the night anywhere on site, like tents?
- Do the logistics work for what you want to achieve and accomplish?
- Where can you park?
- Is there an electrical supply for entertainment
- Ask yourself if all the basic amenities and technical arrangements take care of.
- Are there any restrictions on noise?

**Overall:**

Whether you are having an indoor or outdoor wedding, let's check over the finer things you might want to ask just so you are clear and both singing from the same hymn sheet!

You also may just want clarification that you are on the right track.

Don't forget to get it all in writing, so you have proof, just in case. You never know what you might need it to refer to.

**Ask yourself:**

- Does it match us and our theme?
- Are we within budget?
- Is it big enough?
- Does it logistically work?
- Are all amenities met?

**To check with the venue:**

- What does the price include? Ask for a breakdown.
- What are the catering choices
- Are there wine and drink options?
- Do they have any exclusive packages that include certain arrangements?
- What decorations are you allowed to do?
- Are the table linens, chairs, and tables included?
- Are there any floral arrangements included?
- Are they licensed for ceremonies, whether it's indoor or outdoor?
- Do they recommend any suppliers?

Have fun investigating your venue choices. Take it all in. Take notes and pictures for inspiration on your phone so that you can reflect once you're home with your feet up with a brew, or when your out with friends, you can divulge everything you've come across.

**Notes:**

# Registrar/celebrant/humanist

## Registrar.

A registrar is an employee of the local authority. They can conduct legally binding marriages and civil partnerships; they can do this in registry offices and any building or space that is licensed for civil weddings.

You can organise your registrar by contacting the local authority in the district you are about to marry.

Two registrars are sometimes used for a civil marriage or civil partnership, one will conduct the ceremony, and the other will get you and your witnesses to sign the registration document.

The fee of a registrar will depend on the premises used and the district your ceremony will take place in.

## Celebrant.

A celebrant is someone who can perform your wedding in a non-religious way. They can create a more bespoke, meaningful ceremony.

A good independent celebrant will spend time with you both, ask you lots of questions about you, your lives together, your relationship, and all the different aspects, and they will work with you to create your unique love story. They will put this into words, illustrations, and memories to share with your guests for your ceremony. Moreover, they will lead the service in this manner, so it's special and meaningful to you both.

Celebrants can lead your ceremony in any place, location, or time. They can do it in any style or format you want.

They will also help you choose the order of your ceremony, the words, music, and rituals you would like. They will help you put together specific celebrations for you both, such as handfasting, candle ceremonies, and if there is something of significance and specific from your culture.

**Things for you to know:**

- A celebrant must have two documents in order to conduct ceremonies. Please ask if they have them, one is a combined declaration of no impediment, and the other is a marriage certificate.
- Make sure they are insured.
- A celebrant-led ceremony is not a legally binding agreement. You will still need to go to the registry office and complete your official marriage for it to be legal in England and Wales.

**Humanist.**

It's your wedding, your way with a humanist ceremony. The ceremonies are non-religious, inclusive, and personally tailored to you.

If you want to hold your wedding outdoors, from an intimate garden affair, a woodland wonderland wedding to a beachfront beauty ceremony, you name it; they can do it.

Humanist ceremonies offer meaningful and tailor-made marriages, usually in any location and style, giving you a chance to have the wedding you've always wanted.

If you don't want to exchange rings, then don't. On the other hand, if you want lots of singing in your ceremony, do it. Whatever is true to you both is accommodated.

Humanist ceremonies are led by trained and accredited celebrants.

**Things to know:**

Humanist marriages are only legal in Scotland, Northern Ireland, Jersey, and Guernsey.

They are not legal in England or Wales.

You will have to register your marriage, attend the registry office, and go through the legalities for it to be recognised. You can do this before or after your humanist wedding.

Make sure you see their celebrant certificates and their insurance.

**Notes:**

# Commitment ceremony/Elopements/Blessings

## What is a commitment ceremony?

A commitment ceremony is not legally binding. And they are not allowed to be held in churches. You can declare your love for each other, celebrate your relationship, express your commitment to each other, vow to spend the rest of your lives together in front of your loved ones, and celebrate just like any other wedding. Still, you just won't be legally married.

No matter what relationship you have, anyone can have a commitment ceremony.

It allows you to exchange rings still and make all the promises you want for each other, to each other.

Contact your local authority for approved celebrants that can hold your commitment ceremony. Or, as it's not legally binding, a family member or friend could lead your ceremony if you prefer that.

You don't need a licensed premise to hold a commitment ceremony. You could do it in your back garden, your local field, beach, or anywhere you fancy, as it's not legally binding, and you are not tied to using certain premises. You may need permission from the landowner if it's not your land, though.

Anything goes with a commitment ceremony. You could write your own vows, write promises to each other, or choose readings or poems for people to read out during your ceremony. These could have special meaning to each of you. There is no limit.

Your commitment rings could take the form of a traditional wedding ring, a personalised or unusual ring, a ring tattoo, or something similar to an engagement ring, whatever is suitable for you.

Stay true to yourselves as anything goes!

### Elopement:

Are you looking at symbolising your marriage with just the 2 of you (plus witnesses), or maybe even just you and close family members or friends, maybe even without anyone's knowledge? Eloping is a meaningful, legal alternative to the big white wedding.

If you don't want to do the traditional wedding, eloping to your ideal destination is a fun option that does not involve many people. There are no rules regarding location; as long as you follow the marriage rules of the country you wed in and follow their legal requirements for marrying, you are good to go.

Traditional weddings tend to focus on the guests and their experience, but an elopement focuses on both of you.

### Positives for eloping;

- It will save you a lot of money
- Avoids family politics
- Traditional weddings just make no sense to you
- You don't like planning
- You are marrying later in life or for the 2nd time
- With the money you save on the wedding, you could go on an all-out no holes barred honeymoon!

- Until you tell people, it's just your special secret
- You still want it to be a legal marriage.

## Things you still need to know;

- In the UK, you still need to notify the registry office 29 days before you wed, this includes giving them the details of the venue where you intend to wed, so it's not as spontaneous as it once was historically but still special
- You still need to book a registrar to conduct it legally in England and Wales
- You can still do it in a Church of England. The notice of marriage doing it this way is having your banns read
- You can give notice outside of the UK as long as your partner is a British citizen and the country is part of the British Subjects Facilities Act
- You need parental permission if under 18 in certain countries
- You will need 2 witnesses still
- If you're eloping abroad, you still have to abide by the legal laws of marriage for that country for it to be a legal marriage
- You don't have to do the suit n wedding dress combo. You could do it in your Sunday best, beachwear, fancy dress, whatever suits you both
- Remember, it's your chance to do it your way. Make it count

## Do's and don'ts:

- Do reveal your news to your families. They will want to hear you're married from yourselves and not from social media

- Do prepare yourself for adverse reactions once friends and family have heard the news. You don't need to justify yourself to anyone, but just be prepared for some upset or shock

- Do remember to find out if you need witnesses, as some, say, overseas chapels provide witnesses. Some may allow you to get anyone off the street, but that may be risky. In other places, you will need to bring witnesses with you for it to be a legal marriage

- Do use a planning service if your idea is to elope in a different country and if you can afford it, as no one will know the lay of the land more so than a wedding planner in that local area. Either that or do your research

- Don't forget a photographer, or maybe designate one of your witnesses to take photographs of you both on your elopement day

- Don't just turn up on the day. Maybe go and meet your suppliers, venue, choice of country, etc., before your day. It will make you feel more at ease and comfortable in your choices

- Don't expect gifts. It should go without saying, really

**Eloping history:**

Elope/Eloping: to run away secretly in order to get married

Centuries ago, it was forbidden for anyone to marry in England and Wales without their parent's permission under the age of 21. So the young and in love would travel to the borders of Scotland, where it was much easier to marry. The first town over the border became a haven for young lovers to marry secretly. This town was and is Gretna Green. Since 1754 people have been eloping here to marry their loved ones, and still, to this day, it is a romantic destination for a wedding. Steeped in all the history, it truly brings the magic for a truly special day.

## Marriage blessings:

A blessing is a spiritual way of symbolising the strength of your commitment to each other, and newlyweds can be blessed as part of their marriage. Usually, it takes place after the official part of your wedding. Couples already married can also be blessed in church even if they got married in the UK or abroad.

It is not an actual marriage service. No banns, exchange of rings, or signing of the register are required if the blessing is held separately from your wedding.

You can be blessed in any church of your choice.

A blessing is not legally binding.

A blessing ceremony is great for people that want to be blessed religiously but cannot get married in a religious ceremony due to not being able to marry in a church. For example, you've been divorced before, and your church forbids religious marriages for divorced people.

A blessing can be designed similarly to a wedding with hymns, readings, and bell ringing. You could go all out and be charged accordingly, or you could have a small intimate, low-key service.

After all, it's all about acknowledging your commitment and asking for God's blessing and guidance in your life together.

Blessings can also be non-religious. They are less formal, the wordings are adapted to non-religious associations, and they can be held in any venue, with a celebrant or humanist to lead the ceremony.

Happy blessings!

**Notes:**

# Vows/Handfasting/Signing of the register

**Vows:**

Vows: a solemn promise

dedicate to someone or something

This is your chance, and these are the words said to each other that express both your intentions and your promise to each other during your marriage. You can go into how you intend to navigate your path of life together and what meaning you intend to give your marriage.

Your wedding vows reveal a lot about your true intentions for your marriage. So here are a few tips to get you in the vow writing mood if your choosing to write your own vows.

You could even surprise your partner by saying your own vows to them without their knowledge. What a gift to your loved one.

**Vow writing tips:**

- What do you expect from your future together? Tip, "I promise to always be there for you, always support you, and cheer you on."
- How much do you love them? Tip, "I promise to always be there for you; through all life's ups and downs, I will always be by your side no matter what."

- Writing your vows is writing a promise to your partner of what you want to bring to your marriage and what you see happening in your future. Tip, "I vow always to be faithful and to always be by your side."
- Write what you are grateful for.
- Write about what they bring to your table, the meaningful, the funny, the pleasurable.
- Do not talk about your ex-partners, do not swear or talk about sex or anything gross, or discuss your partner's weaknesses or vulnerabilities. Please let common sense prevail.
- It's not war and peace. You only need to be writing around 6 vows/promises.
- Be meaningful.

And if you don't fancy writing and saying your own vows in front of everybody, then there are always the traditional ones. No pressure.

## 7 vows of marriage:

The traditional vow recital

I, ———, take you, ————, to be my (wife/husband), to have and to hold, from this day forward, for better for worse, for richer, for poorer, in sickness and in health, to love and cherish always.

## Handfasting:

"tying the knot. "

Handfasting ceremonies have been around since Ancient times and holds, a time-honoured tradition for showing an act of commitment and unity. More commonly used in Wiccan and Pagan ceremonies, but anyone can take part in this tradition nowadays.

Traditionally a couple would be brought together to have a braided cord or ribbon tied around their hands in the presence of a priest/celebrant whilst explaining the ritual and what it means to you both to your guests. It shows that you are binding your lives together and that the union of your hopes and desires is tied together, joining both hands to symbolise your free will to enter into the marriage. Next, the celebrant/priest would read the vows as the cords wrapped and entwined around your hands, joining you together. Once completed, then they will explain what the commitment symbolises. Once you are bound together, you can exchange additional vows to each other, or you could use the handfasting ceremony as your vows and then go onto the ring exchange.

For a more earthy look, why not have a natural garland, as grape vines or flowers weaved together for your handfasting cord?

If you want to do some other form of meaning for your handfasting ceremony, may I suggest colour-coordinating the braided cords or ribbon? You could do white for purity, blue for fidelity, and red for passion. It will make a lovely keepsake for after your wedding too. You can get your guests to write messages on your ribbon as a nice keepsake too.

The handfasting part of the ceremony is not legally binding on its own if you want to use it as part of a blessing or ritual, and anyone can perform it.

If you want to use the handfasting as part of a church ceremony, it would be down to the discretion of your clergyman.

However, some celebrants/registrars will be qualified to do the handfasting as part of a civil ceremony.

**The signing of the register:**

After your wedding ceremony, your marriage must be entered in the marriage register to be legal. You both must sign it, plus 2 witnesses and the person that conducted the ceremony.

**Witnesses:**

- Check with the registry office about witness age limits in the district you're getting married in, as not all countries have the same limitations
- Witnesses must understand the language that is being used in the ceremony
- Witnesses must be of sound mind and be able to understand what is taking place
- The registry office staff are not allowed to act as witnesses

Before you sign on the dotted line, please ensure all the information is correct on your register because getting this changed after signing and receiving your marriage certificate is a nightmare. You have to provide evidence and proof of the changes and explain in writing how the register came to be incorrect in the first place. This process can take a very long time, so check it before you sign it.

**Notes:**

# Wedding traditions/wedding etiquette

"something old, something new, something borrowed, something blue, and a silver sixpence in your shoe."

For years, different cultures have created their wedding customs and superstitions. Many of these have stood the test of time and evolved into the wedding traditions we know and love today. Some people like to keep the tradition alive and will keep the tradition going, and some may want to modernise it to suit their way of thinking and bring it into the year we are now, so let's delve into the hidden meanings of these traditions, and take from it what you will.

### Something old:

Traditionally it provides protection for the bride's eventual baby.

This will stem from your family and their past. Maybe it will entail a piece of family jewellery or a grandmother's wedding dress.

### Something new:

Representing good fortune and success in the bride's new life.

This could be a new wedding dress or perhaps new bridal shoes. It could also be a gift from your partner or one of the bride's family members.

**Something borrowed:**

Meaning to transfer another happy bride's luck to the new bride's relationship. Reminding the bride that her family and friends will be there for her when help is needed.

This could be a family veil, a handbag, a handkerchief, or even a hairpin.

**Something blue:**

To thwart the evil eye, it symbolises faithfulness and loyalty. When blue represented purity.

The garter is often recommended for your something blue. Or maybe a piece of blue jewellery.

**Sixpence in her shoe:**

A symbol of prosperity and happiness for the new couple. Traditionally given to the bride for good luck and to attract wealth. Believed to be most effective if it was placed in her shoe by her father, meaning he had sent the couple his good wishes.

Done altogether, a bride who does all 5 things has the ingredients for a successful marriage.

**Why do we do what we do?**

**The down-on-one-knee proposal.**

Traditionally men would bend down in front of the woman they loved. And in some religions kneeling in front of someone shows respect, loyalty, and obedience.

Fast forward to now, some people still get down on one knee to propose.

It represents a somewhat vulnerable and emotional connection, showing your partner that you are willing to commit the rest of your life to them, giving them what they need and want.

It's like you are surrendering to your love.

How romantic!


**You must not see each other the night before your wedding.**

If you go back in time to when marriages were arranged. The couple was not allowed to see each other before the marriage took place for fear that they would pull out of it. So they didn't meet until they saw each other at the altar.

In today's society, it's simply seen as bad luck to see your other half on the morning of your wedding. However, some people still choose to do this tradition to build up the excitement for the day's proceedings and to give their partner a surprise at the altar with how stunning they look.

You will want to rest up and be prepared. Whether you stay together or not, it's up to you.


**Why do you get given away?**

Back in the days when marriages were more like an arrangement again, brides would literally be handed over, usually by their father, to their new owner, in exchange for money or a dowry.

Now, it doesn't matter who "gives you away." It can be a special moment between you and your dad, or mum or sibling. Whatever you're comfortable with.

**Standing on the left of the groom.**

This comes from an age when men wore swords on their person.

Traditionally the man would need to protect his bride with his left arm and use his sword with his right to fight off unwarranted attention from family members.

This tradition has never changed as brides/grooms still to this day stand to the left of their partner. There are just no swords nowadays.

**Asking permission for their hand in marriage?**

Historically with the woman being the 'property' of the man of the house, it was always expected that the male (groom) would ask permission to propose from the man of the house (usually the father) for the lady's hand in marriage.

Families nowadays still expect the question to be asked.

My advice, use your judgment on the family dynamics. If in doubt, just ask the question. Maybe use this time and get both of your parents together to discuss your question and use the time to get to know one another more.

**Wearing pearls is bad luck!**

In ancient, medieval history, wearing pearls on your wedding day represented the tears that you would shed during your marriage.

Pearls are a timeless accessory, and if they happen to be part of your something old or borrowed, surely that balances out the superstition?

## Taking the married name?

Traditionally the woman took the man's surname after marriage as she belonged to him now.

Changing your surname in marriage is less common now, but millions of newly married couples still stick to this tradition. Whatever your preference is, I suppose.

## The garter throw!

This tradition began a very, very long time ago when it was considered good luck for guests to take home a piece of the bride's clothing. So, family and guests would follow the bride and groom up to their chambers after their wedding and try and rip a "lucky" piece of clothing off the bride's wedding dress. It soon turned into a bride wearing a garter, the only item removed to protect the bride from overzealous guests hurting her by ripping and removing clothing.

It was also seen as a consummation of marriage that a groom would present the garter to family and friends after their first night together as man and wife.

In more modern days, the "garter race" was formed, where groomsmen would race to the bridal home of the newlyweds. After the wedding, the winner of the race would be rewarded with the bride's garter, which he would pin to his hat for good luck.

Now in modern times, the groom has the privilege of removing the garter at the wedding reception, he then tosses it to the unmarried male guests at the wedding, and the one who catches it, it is thought to bring them good luck and means that he would be married next. This man is then supposed to put it on the left leg of the unmarried girl who caught the bouquet!

Matchmaking at its best.

**Carrying the bride over the threshold.**

Many moons ago, it was feared that evil spirits lurked on the threshold of newlyweds' houses, and the power would destroy a marriage and its ability for the wife to bear children.

So, for this reason, the man would make sure that the bride didn't touch the ground as they entered over the threshold.

Nowadays, it's just fun to do.

**Receiving a horseshoe on your wedding day.**

The horseshoe is a symbol of good luck, and receiving one from a female family member is meant to bring you good luck in your marriage and good luck in fertility.

The horseshoe has been a sign of luck from as early as the 8th century, with its crescent shape representing various moon goddesses, protecting against the curse of the evil eye.

It's not as common to see horseshoes at your wedding anymore, but if you're attracted to nostalgia, this one certainly cannot harm you.

No matter what traditions you decide to follow, remember that it's your wedding, and it's all about you both.

Traditions back in the day were for brides and grooms, so if you are hosting a same-sex wedding, there are many fun ideas to replace these with if it's not for you, or just adapt them to yourselves. Put a modern spin on things.

Set a new tradition and have fun.

Happy planning.

### Wedding etiquette.

Traditional weddings have a lot more formalities/expectations, with more things to remember. Still, nowadays, people who get married are choosing to do things more their own way, and for them to be not as formal, it is totally up to you how you choose your day to run. But here is an insight as to what traditional formalities/expectations look like and see if they can be adapted to you in any way, you never know. You may want to keep some of them too.

### Announcing your engagement/marriage in the newspaper.

Traditionally, the bride's father would announce his daughter's engagement in the newspaper, but nothing is stopping you from doing this too. If you want to announce it all to the world, here is what would traditionally be said.

"The engagement is announced between David, youngest son of Mr. and Mrs. Michael Wood of Blackpool, Lancashire, and Elizabeth, only daughter of Mr. and Mrs. Paul Harvey of Preston, Lancashire."

Similar wordings would go into announcing your marriage, too, but it would also have the date of your marriage and the church details too.

It does make a nice keepsake for your bridal scrapbook if you like to treasure things like this.

Not a formality now these days, though.

Nowadays, people tend to go straight for social media to announce anything major that happens in their lives, but before you hit post! You might want to tell your close family and friends your good news before you shout it from the rooftops, save any upset.

**Guest list and who to invite!**

This has got to be one of the most difficult parts of wedding planning, who to invite. Here are a few hints and tips to try and help you along your way.

- If they are invited to the hen or stag, then they should probably be invited to your wedding.
- You do not have to add a single guest plus 1, especially if you have never met them. It is an outdated tradition nowadays.
- You would, however, invite your friend's long-term partner, especially if you have met them and you are friendly. If your budget doesn't stretch just be consistent with your choices and don't deviate from your plan, as you don't want to offend anyone.

- If your parents are footing the bill for the wedding, then it's probably only fair and polite that they invite some of their friends to your wedding. However, if you are paying and your parents are adding up the numbers, and it's going over your budget, maybe explain to your parents that you simply cannot afford these extras when they are not your friends. It's your day.

Remember, it's your wedding, and if your budget doesn't stretch, then as long as you've told people beforehand why certain things can't happen, they can't be disappointed. You can't invite every Tom, Dick, and Harry. There has to be a line drawn somewhere.

**Who walks down the aisle first?**

Traditionally the bride and her father would walk down the aisle first, leading the way for her bridesmaids, flower girls, and pageboys.

Now it is nice either way. Maybe your flower girl drops petals down the aisle for you to walk on, or your bridesmaids are needed at the back to hold your train on your dress. So it seems, either way, would work.

**Receiving line.**

This is when the hosts of the wedding and the bridal party would line up at the dining hall entrance and shake hands and welcome all the guests one by one.

People tend to prefer to circulate between themselves now, giving it a much more personal touch, don't you think?

## Seating arrangements.

The married couple should always be sat together in the centre of the top table, and traditionally the top table should look like below:

| Chief | Father of the | Mother of the | Groom | Bride | Father of the | Mother of the | Bestman |
|-------|---------------|---------------|-------|-------|---------------|---------------|---------|
| B/maid | Groom | Bride | | | Bride | Groom | |

But with some families having tricky situations, this can be hard to manage. Maybe you want to extend your top table to include others, and possibly your parents would like to host their own table, leaving you 2 with your friends on your head table, or maybe you just have a table for 2 at the top and save the drama. It's your day, don't forget.

## Bridal party.

Ushers, the floor managers for the day, choose wisely. They should ensure the guests are in the right place at the right time for the ceremony, wedding reception, and other arrangements unless you have no formal seating plan and it's free for all.

They set the tone for the day and are the first thing guests see. So make sure they have good manners too.

- Pageboys or the best man are the ring bearers usually.
- Flower girls, your cute petal droppers usually.
- Bridesmaids are your wing women.
- The chief bridesmaid or maid of honour is the head of your bridesmaids.

Happy choosing.

**Notes;**

# Speeches/Guest etiquette

## Speeches

Out of all the traditions and the things you should or should not do, speeches are probably the most nerve-wracking. The speeches tend to happen once the guests are all seated and about to start the wedding meal, or they are done after the meal, but before the cake cutting, my guess is most people would prefer to get them over and done with so they can enjoy the rest of the day and if tradition rules the speeches should go in this order;

### Bride's father

He generally talks about his daughter- hopefully nothing too embarrassing- welcoming the new husband into the family, thanking all that have come to the wedding, and toasting the bride and groom on their health and happiness together.

### Groom

This speech is on behalf of himself and the bride. It starts with responding to the bride's father, thanking him for his welcome, and how much they have supported your unison and plans towards their wedding, also thanking his own parents too, thanks guests for coming and for their gifts. Also, names any guests that have not managed to join the celebration due to illness and sends them well wishes.

He also gives a toast to the bridesmaids, thanks them for all they have done, and hands out gifts to the bridesmaids, best men, ushers, and all who have helped with the wedding preparations.

Best-man

This speech is on behalf of himself, the ushers, and the bridesmaids. Starts with thanking the bride and groom and replying to anything the groom said in his speech that needed answering. Then it's over to the best man, really. This could be very funny or painful depending on the groom's choice of best man really, so choose well.

It ends with a toast to the happy couple.

Gifts for the mums are a great idea, whether that's flowers, jewellery, or writing them a thank you note from the heart. That always goes down well, and especially for any family members that have helped do anything for the wedding it is a good idea to thank them too, maybe your Aunt made the cake for instance. The groom needs to be handing these out at his speech time.

No one else is required to give a speech, but if anyone wishes to speak, it should be welcomed.

Not to break tradition, but more and more brides are choosing to stand up and have their say at their wedding celebration too, so if you fancy grabbing the mic, just do it and have fun!

**Guest etiquette;**

What is the done thing at weddings? Let's break it down into what guests expect from you as a couple and the do's and don'ts of guests, and their behaviour at weddings. Simple.

## What do guests expect?

Guests will have a lot of questions and queries about your wedding, whether it's about transportation if you're at different venues, allergies to the menus, the dress code, etc. Save yourself the awkward phone calls, stress, and anxiety during your planning by making certain that all the possible information a guest might need is given to them, so it avoids unnecessary questions. Maybe use a wedding website or page that all guests can access so all helpful information can be easily uploaded for guests ahead of schedule. Maybe designate your chief bridesmaid to run it for you, collate all the information for you, and respond to any queries there.

Remember that not all of your guests need to be invited to the full day. You can just invite guests to your evening celebration, especially if space is tight due to the size of the venue or your budget is nearing its peak. Gone are the days when you must invite everyone you've ever known. Take your time. Planning the guest list can be tricky, even without extra family dynamics too.

Try and get around all your guests, chat with them, and thank them for coming. They will really appreciate that you've made an effort for them, and they will remember that moment and treasure it, and so will you.

It's up to you how you want to word your invitations. Back in the day, the brides' parents would invite the guests, so they would word the invites, but nowadays, it's acceptable for your invitations to come from yourselves. Your stationery person will have a load of templates and wording styles for you to choose from.

If your guests don't RSVP, just chase up with them for your confirmation, their response could have gotten lost in the post, or they might have thought they'd replied when they hadn't. Anything really, and it beats them actually turning up on the day when you'd presumed they weren't coming and not booked them a seat. Always best for you to double-check.

Keep everyone in the loop as much as they need to be to make things easier on yourself.

**Do's and Don'ts for guests;**

**Do's**

- Be in the moment, be an active participant in their wedding
- Send your reply back asap, whether by post, email, or on their website
- Check out their wedding website, and tell them your dietary requirements asap
- Choose a gift from their gift registry
- Check the dress code. If there is no dress code, treat it as a formal occasion
- Follow the rules of social media and photographs
- Respect the couple. It's their day, not yours
- Stick to the seating plan if there is one
- Introduce yourself to guests, sign the guest book, and socialise responsibly
- Use your manners. They are free
- If the couple requests it, limit your phone use
- If you're invited to both the ceremony and the reception, go to both. It's not optional
- Arrive early to the ceremony

## Don'ts

- Don't reply to your invite and leave a voicemail. These get lost; make sure you speak to someone so they know you're attending if you're phoning the reply through

- If you're single, don't assume you will get a plus 1, and if you don't, it's rude to ask for one, so don't bother just enjoy being there yourself

- Do not wear white, ivory, or any shade of both colours. Leave that to the bride

- Do not try and outshine the bride and groom, don't propose on someone else's wedding day. It is a tad inconsiderate, don't you think

- Try and refrain from posting all over social media before the bride and groom have even done the honours. They might not want to share their special day with everyone on the internet, and especially do not share pictures of the cute children without getting permission to do so from the parents first. If you are unsure as to whether to post anything, maybe wait and see if the bride and groom post anything first.

- Don't wear jeans to a wedding unless it's a cowboy theme, that is

- If your child's name is not on the invite, then you can presume that children are not invited to the wedding, don't just "take them along."

- It is polite to bring the happy couple a gift on their wedding day, don't worry if everything is out of your price range on their gift list. As long as you don't bring some random and inappropriate gift, I am sure it will be fine. They will know you've made an effort.

- Don't show up late to the wedding
- Don't give a drunk speech. You will totally regret it, don't just wing it either; go prepared
- As fun as it is to dance on the tables, unless the bride and groom are doing it, please refrain yourself. Don't do a striptease on the dance floor. If you wouldn't want someone doing that at your wedding, don't make it ok to do it at someone else's.

At the end of the day, be respectful and gracious. The happy couple has spent months, if not years, planning this day, preparing for every eventuality, it's been their labour of love, and they want you there to share it with them. Enjoy it!

**Notes;**

# Dates, days & seasons

## What's in a day?

"Monday for health, Tuesday for wealth, Wednesday's the best of all. Thursday brings crosses, And Friday losses, But Saturday - no luck at all."

"If you marry in Lent, you're sure to repent."

"To marry during a full moon is unlucky, and during Lent is poor choice."

"It has been said that the happy couple should exchange vows as the clocks hand is ascending towards heaven (upwards)."

"Friday the 13th is a day of bad luck, and 31st of October, well, it's Halloween."

Traditions, superstitions, old wives tales, most of these sayings, rhymes, and beliefs were made in ancient times when they were meant to ward off evil spirits and bring luck to the newly married couple. In this day and age, they are probably nothing more than a myth.

You will probably find that the 13th of the month and the 31st of October are the last days to get booked up, so if you're looking to get married quicker,

I bet you could get it at a steal on those days. Imagine the fun of getting married on Halloween.

Nowadays, you will probably find Monday to Thursday weddings are less expensive, Friday being attractive as it's the start of the weekend, Saturday and Sunday being your more expensive days to get married on, simply because more people are off work on those days, so it's more appealing to engaged couples.

According to astrology, it is not appropriate to get married in your birthday month as it can make a person self-centred.

Chinese philosophy says that the number 9 is very lucky, as it's pronounced the same as the word "long-lasting" some people get married on the 9th, 19th, or 29th, just in the hope that their marriage endures.

**My advice:**

Go with whatever feels right for you both. Trust in your instincts.

**"Marry when the year is new and he'll be loving, kind and true, When February birds do mate, you wed not or dread your fate. If you wed when March winds blow, joy and sorrow you'll both know. Marry in April when you can, and joy for maiden and for man. Marry in the month of May and you'll live to rue the day. Marry when June roses grow and over land and sea you'll go. Those in July who do wed must labour for their daily bread. Whoever wed in August be many a change is sure to see. Marry in September's shrine your living will be rich and fine. If October you do marry, love will come but riches tarry. If you wed in bleak November, only joys will come, remember. When December snow falls fast, marry and true love will last."**

In Roman times, it was the animal mating season in May, their feast of the dead, and the festival of the Goddess of chastity, both being in May, hence why they thought it was an unlucky month for marriages. Team that with people only having their annual bath in May, people tended to smell a lot better in June. Even Queen Victoria didn't allow her children to marry in May. Ancient history now, though.

Fast forward to today, the most popular months to get married are from May to October, so not so superstitious now.

**Spring:**

New beginnings and transformations, this is the season that says, start fresh and start over.

**Summer:**

Represents optimism, positives, hope for the future, and joy. Summer is life and the endless opportunities that await.

**Autumn:**

Symbolic of abundance, plenty, ripening, and harvest.

**Winter:**

A period of self-reflection and preparation for the new beginnings ahead. Symbolising a period of quiet reflection.

What do the seasons represent to you? Did you always dream of a winter wonderland wedding?   Whatever month you marry in, it has to be true to you both, and I would say that if numerology, astrology, family traditions, or anything that you look for guidance and intuition, look to that rather than the out-of-date old wives tales. Happy choosing.

**Notes;**

# Rings and meanings

### Engagement/Wedding/Eternity

The 3 rings, your engagement ring represents the love and promise to get married. The wedding ring symbolises your eternal love, commitment to each other, and the coming together of your union. The 3rd ring represents a large milestone for you both as a couple, whether that's an anniversary or the birth of your first child.

### Why the 4th finger on the left hand?

It's believed that this tradition comes from the Romans again when they believed a vein ran straight from the 4th finger on the left hand to the heart. Although some may say now that the left hand is used less and so it's more practical to adorn your rings on that hand, personally, I like the romance of the 1st explanation.

They do say that the wedding band should be the first ring on the finger to ensure its proper position closest to the heart. So on your wedding day, move your engagement ring to your right hand, then return it to your left hand after your nuptials to go over your wedding band.

Either that or remove your engagement ring altogether and leave it at home. It's up to you.

# What's in a jewel?

Jewels and gems have symbolic meanings that can spell either triumph or trouble for your marriage if it features in either your engagement ring or wedding band.

## Sapphire

Traditionally means honesty, sincerity, and faithfulness. It is believed to provide good fortune within a marriage, to keep it strong and healthy.

## Aquamarine

Representing marital harmony, ensuring a long and happy marriage.

## Pearl

Traditions state it rings of bad luck as its shape is like a tear. But symbolises loyalty and integrity.

## Ruby

Signifies the passion within, bringing strength, courage, and love to nurture in a marriage.

## Emerald

Shows intent for a happy and blessed marriage, bringing luck, love, peace, and hope to your marriage.

## Diamond

An engagement ring with a diamond signifies shared happiness in your married life, a symbol of sincere love that will last forever.

## Amethyst

Bringing faithfulness, love, patience, and peace to you both.

## Topaz

Balance your emotions, bringing strength, longevity, and wisdom to oneself.

## Garnet

The commitment stone symbolises perseverance and strength, renowned for being the symbol of life.

Maybe the choice for you is your birthstone? These gemstones represent a person's period of birth, usually the month or the zodiac sign. Giving the ring a more meaningful representation, don't you think?

January = Garnet

February = Amethyst

March = Aquamarine

April = Diamond

May = Emerald

June = Pearl

July = Ruby

August = Peridot

September = Sapphire

October = Opal

November = Golden Topaz

December = Turquoise


## How do you choose the right ring?

- Choose the shape ( wishbone, oval, square etc.)
- Choose the metal for the band
- What size gem do you want
- Get the measurements right
- How will the engagement ring look next to the wedding ring
- Buy a certified ring
- Be smart about the quality and the cut of the ring


## The metal band.


## Silver

A symbol of prosperity.


**Gold**

The classic


**Platinum**

A rarer precious metal


With the demands of day-to-day life, buying an 18ct, 14ct, or 9ct gold wedding ring is more suited to now. Try and match the skin tone, maybe. People with cool skin tones benefit from white metals such as silver, platinum, or white gold. And for people with warmer skin tones, the gold coppery colours look beautiful with their complexion. Have fun choosing, though.


**Alternatives to rings;**

Is jewellery not your thing? Then what about matching tattoos on your ring fingers? Maybe solid black lines, your partner's initials, and meaningful images that represent you both. Your ring, your way. His and hers watches may be engraved with messages on them both from each other. Signature bracelets or necklaces. Wood and silicone rings are another alternative to metal bands, something to keep in mind. If jewellery is truly not your thing, there is always something else as long as it fits in with you both.

**Notes;**

# Food/favours/cake

Choosing your wedding food can maybe feel overwhelmed by the dishes you've seen hundreds of times. You want something memorable and special for your first meal as a wedded couple, aka the wedding breakfast.

If you are celebrating in a venue, they may have certain catering policies and packages. Ask your venue about these, they may have in-house catering services that you are required to use, or they may charge you a fee if you want to bring someone else in.

If you choose a package with your venue, they may offer you a wedding taster session, which would be great for you to help choose your menu for your wedding meal. Working closely with your venue, they need to ensure that you are comfortable with your wedding menu options. You need to tell them about any dietary requirements that need accommodating, and you can work out any seasonal selections, if anything needs to be presented in a certain way, and if anything is to be served in a certain way too. The wedding breakfast is about 1.5 - 2 hours, depending on your speeches and how lengthy they are.

Usually, food choices with a venue consist of the following:
- canapés for when you first arrive at the venue, if you are marrying elsewhere, or just after your ceremony while you're circulating if you are marrying at the venue, charged per head, usually 3 or 4 different varieties
- wedding breakfast usually consists of a starter, main course, dessert, tea, and coffee, charged per head

- evening buffet for your evening guests as well as your day guests, charged per head

If you're having a wedding with a venue but in a different style, maybe you could work alongside them with your catering options and still offer different menu options for you and your guests. Maybe you have a later ceremony so you won't need the wedding breakfast and the evening buffet? Maybe it's a non-formal affair, and you want more of an afternoon tea option for you and your guests. Maybe consider a hot/cold buffet as a menu option, where guests choose their own food, and work alongside your venue and the catering options, so you choose the right wedding menu for you and your guests.

Having a wedding that you're organising the food for separately with outside caterers may become a bit of a headache. How do you choose what food to serve? Here are a few ideas for you; get creative

- How about asking your family or friends about their favourite food or meals? That may shed some inspiration for you as menu options. Maybe choose 1 from one side of the family and 1 from the other side of the family, so at your wedding, you can combine a family recipe from each side of the family. Serving them both on your day to solidify your joining of 2 families.

- Maybe base your wedding menu on your favourite foods, you like to dine in certain restaurants and you have a favourite dish that is your go-to dish?

- Can you remember what you served at your engagement party? Maybe use a dish from that menu and relive it at your wedding breakfast, personalises your menu

- the most important thing is, is that you tailor your wedding menu to you both and your taste

- work with your caterer to devise a menu that is both delicious and meaningful

Maybe you're having an outdoor ceremony, and you have food trucks there instead of caterers. Your guests can have the experience of choosing their own food as to what they fancy on the day. Here are some suggestions for food trucks

- Wood-fired pizza
- BBQ station, burgers
- Hot dog cart
- Fish and chip van
- Roast hog on a spit roast
- Street food vans
- Taco van
- Dessert truck
- Ice cream cart
- Popcorn cart
- Candy floss cart
- Cheese station

Whatever you have chosen for your wedding ceremony, indoors, outdoors, late ceremony, full day, consider your options, catering services or in-house services. Selecting the food should be a fun experience. During tasting sessions, let your taste buds do the talking, and don't forget any dietary restrictions for yourself or any guests.

**Favours:**

Giving guests something to remember from your wedding day in the form of a wedding favour has been around for hundreds of years.

Traditionally guests were given 5 sugar-coated sugar almonds. These symbolise health, wealth, fertility, happiness, and long life.

Not many couples stick to this now, adapting their favours for something more in keeping with their wedding and theme.

Here are a few more commonly used favour ideas for you:
- Flower seeds so your guests can plant something in their garden to remember your day by
- Mini bottles of spirits, maybe one for the men and a different one for the ladies. You could even locally source these if you marry in an area that makes local produce
- if you want to put your own stamp on things at your own wedding, maybe you could make your own DIY food wedding favours
- lottery tickets for all adults
- a little scented candle or a little scented bar of soap make quirky favours
- a cone of pick-n-mix sweets, or a wedding biscuit, chocolate truffles, any of these could be wrapped in a lovely cellophane and dressed lovely

Usually, your wedding favours are placed on the tables at each guest's place setting, giving the tables that splash of colour too. Especially if you colour coordinate your favours to your colour scheme, giving that extra touch. Before choosing your favours, maybe consider how they will look on your tables with your other table arrangements.

Wanting to save the pennies and skip the favours? If you do decide this is for you just remind yourself that you are providing drinks, dinner, and desserts for your guests, just in case the guilt creeps in.

## Cake:

Cakes have always had a part to play in a wedding. Initially, guests would bring small cakes and place them in front of the couple. If the couple could successfully kiss over the cakes without knocking them over, they were granted good luck. Today they are mostly served as a sweet treat for the guests and yourselves, obviously.

### Traditions of the wedding cake:

- Wedding cakes were impressive, tiered, white frosted fruitcakes.
- The first cut of the cake made by the bride was to ensure that the marriage would be blessed with children.
- The top tier of the cake was saved for your child's first christening or your first wedding anniversary.
- When cutting the cake, the hand of the groom is placed over the top of the bride, and this shows his support and promise to take care of her and their future.
- Cutting the cake from the bottom tier is a reminder of the relationship's longevity, and this was encouraged to do.

- Each tier of the cake signifies something. The bottom tier is for eating at the ceremony, the middle tier is to give out to your guests, and the top tier is saved.

- Back in the day, there was also a time when there were 2 cakes, a groom's cake being dark and masculine, and a bride's cake in white.

- The tiered shape dates back to the 1755-1812 era, when a London pastry chef modelled his own wedding cake on the steeple of a church in London, inventing the tiered-shaped wedding cake.


**Cake flavours:**

When choosing your wedding cake, make sure you get to taste the flavours from your baker. You should be invited to a cake-tasting session where you can discuss what flavours you would like for your wedding cake. What flavours go with what? What fillings to have, how many tiers, and what design are you looking at? Are you have any decorations on the outside of your cake? Do you need flowers or fruit? There is a lot to discuss other than just how many the cake is for.

Traditionally your cake would be white, but now there is so much more than that involved with a wedding cake, and who is to say that you need to have a traditional cake nowadays anyway, you could have a two-sided cake, one side pretty and feminine and the other side in keeling with your partner, like Spider-Man or something, like with anything, it's your day, go with something that represents you both, but here are a few flavour combinations just to give your taste buds a tingle.

Chocolate cake complemented with buttercream, caramel, raspberry, or mocha filling

Red velvet cake with a cream cheese frosting

Chocolate orange cake with a vanilla buttercream

Carrot cake

Good ol' Victoria sponge

You could always have a mix of fillings instead of a mix of cake flavours, maybe. Just enjoy the cake tasting and go for what feels right.

The cake is cut and served in between dinner and dancing, usually following your first dance. You'll head to cut your cake.

**Don't fancy cake?**

If cake isn't for you, maybe try something different, something that you both like and enjoy. Here are a few ideas for you. The delicious dessert choice is up to you.

- Pie cake, different pie flavours in a tier shape. You could always put a few pickle samples next to your pies so guests can tickle their pickles
- Donut walls displayed uniquely, maybe
- Cheese tower, different cheese wheels all stacked up, maybe served with fruits and pickles, crackers and bread
- Cupcake tower, each guest has an individual cupcake to either eat then or take home

- Chocolate-covered fruit, maybe with a selection of caramels, creams, and sweet sauces
- Cookies and milk
- Cheesecake
- Ice cream cones served with different toppings
- Pancake cakes served with different toppings

Who said your cake had to be cake?

Put a spin on it. If you've got the skills and experience in baking, why not bake your own cake or dessert? It's a pretty big job and not something you want to be doing on your wedding day itself, but in advance, and if you can commit to it and not stress yourself out unduly, why not.

**Notes;**

# Flowers and their meanings

A bride's bouquet is a collection of flowers that the bride holds as she walks down the aisle, adding to the wedding theme and complimenting the wedding dress. A bride's bouquet ties in the wedding design and decor together and would possibly be the first thing the guests see. It's an accessory, a focal point, and plays an important part in the wedding. But...

## Why do we carry a bouquet of flowers?

There are several beliefs regarding carrying flowers down the aisle and why we do it, and it didn't start with flowers. In ancient times, fragrant herbs and spices were carried to ward off bad luck and evil spirits during your wedding. The herbs and spices symbolised the couple's new beginning and brought hope for their future with fertility, happiness and fidelity.

Another reason was that people only had annual baths. Herbs and spices masked bodily odours, so not only were they pretty to look at, they also served a purpose. The herbs and spices that tended to be used were,

- Dill, which is considered to be an aphrodisiac
- Rosemary, representing loyalty
- Wheat, for fertility
- Ivy, representing an unbreakable bond
- Thistle, thyme, heather and basil were used for protection
- Myrtle, considered an ancient symbol of a happy marriage
- English Oak Leaves symbolise the strength and hardiness of love

Brides used flowers to be able to communicate their romantic sentiments by using specific flowers in particular colours, expressing their feelings and emotions through their choice of flower.

All founding factors as to why brides of today carry floral bouquets down the aisle even if it's not for those reasons now and more for decorative purposes.

**Be in the know;**

**Why do we throw the bouquet?**

As it was custom for the groom to throw the garter to his groomsmen (and the male that caught it was apparently the next to marry), the bride threw her bouquet to her bridesmaids (and again who caught it was apparently the next to marry), the groomsman and the bridesmaid that caught the items, were to dance together too at the first dance part of the celebrations. Nowadays, some couples forget this tradition and opt for something else.

If you do not want to throw your bouquet, why not give it to the couple who have attended your wedding and been married the longest, honouring their love and longevity?

Another idea would be to get your florist to make a similar style of the bouquet but a lot smaller in size to throw or use one of your bridesmaid's bouquets as a throwing bouquet. That way, you're not ruining your actual bouquet.

You may want to keep your flowers. You could get them preserved and framed by someone professional.

Press a few flowers from your bouquet, using these in picture frames to decorate your home or putting them in resin to make ornaments for your home too.

Dry the flowers out and make potpourri, or decorate your home with the dried flowers in a vase.

Another alternative would be to keep them in water, feed them flower food, and keep them till they die.


## Who needs flowers?

Traditionally all your guests that attended your ceremony had a flower on their jacket, usually handed out by the ushers at the wedding church or venue. Nowadays, depending on your budget for flowers, it's totally up to you guys how many and who will be needing flowers apart from your bridal party, so here is a brief outline of who needs flowers in your bridal party;

- Bridal bouquet ( hand-tied bouquet, cascade bouquet or teardrop bouquet)
- Maid of Honour bouquet ( hand-tied bouquet, nosegay, posy or wrist corsage)
- Bridesmaids bouquets ( hand-tied bouquet, nosegay, posy or wrist corsage)
- Flower girl ( nosegay, posy, basket of petals, floral wand, or floral crown)
- Grooms boutonnière
- Groomsmen boutonnière, which includes the best man, ushers, page boys, dads
- Mums corsages ( on their jacket, wrist, or handbag)

The bridal bouquet is the main and largest bouquet, consisting of various flowers. Bridesmaids usually have smaller versions of the bride's bouquet, sometimes only having certain flowers in their bouquet, chosen out of the bride's flowers, leaving the bride's bouquet to look slightly different and more elaborate. Depending on their dress colour, you could always have different colours in the bridesmaid's bouquets. For instance, if their dress is blush pink, you probably want to limit the number of pink flowers in their bouquet, so the bouquet contrasts with their dresses.

The groom having his boutonnière as one of the main flowers chosen out of the bride's bouquet, so they match, and the groomsmen adopting for a different flower to match the bridesmaids is a nice way of doing it so it all flows.

Choosing your flowers can go far beyond your roses and peonies; there are tropical flowers for your beach wedding feel, dried flowers for that rustic feel, and artificial flowers for your keepsakes. You could choose your flowers from their meaning and what they represent to you both, or maybe your grandma or mother had certain flowers in their bouquets, and you want to represent a family tradition with your flowers, you could get creative with your colour choices, the list is endless, it's your theme, your wedding.

Remember, if you're planning a summer wedding or getting married in a hot climate, fresh flowers will wilt in the hot sun, so if you want to keep your flowers for after the wedding, make sure you put them into the water after your ceremony and maybe ask your venue to put them in a refrigerator to keep them cool for you.

**Flower choices;**

It may seem like it's a bit of a mind field but a lot of the time, the kind of flowers you choose come down to a few things really,

- personal preference
- the colour theme of your wedding
- the season you are getting married in

There are no right or wrong styles of a bouquet, whether you opt for a traditional cascade bouquet, a rustic dried floral bouquet or a single rose. As long as you are comfortable with your decision and it reflects you both, then go with it.

Before I get onto flowers themselves, the last thing is to make sure your bridal bouquet is proportioned to yourself. You don't want to be swallowed up by something so large or have no impact with something so small. Food for thought.

Now, flowers choices, what do you choose, and what do they mean;

The meaning of each flower is generalised, as the different colours of each flower will have a more solidified meaning about the colour and the flower itself.

**Peony,** with its fluffy petals and large flower head, it's a romantic flower that makes a bold statement. The meaning of a peony is happiness, romance, beauty, honour and love. These flowers come in pink, red, orange, yellow and white colours. They smell divine.

They are seasonal flowers and are not around all year.

**Calla lily,** this delicate, elegant flower grows straight with a trumpet-shaped curl at the tip. Representing a symbol of innocence, purity and admiration. These beautiful flowers come in yellow, orange, white, pink, rose, lavender and dark aubergine. They don't tend to smell much, and certain colours you can get all year round, with some being seasonal colours.

**Rose;** is often the first choice for most couples, with its wide varieties such as tea roses, sweetheart roses, garden roses and spray roses and the fact it is an all-year-round flower. Also, coming in so many colours, it's a beautiful choice. Rose is the symbol of love and purity. Garden roses are the most scented, with the other roses having a more subtle scent. You will be spoilt for choice of colours. They are white, ivory, cream, yellow, lemon, green, orange, peach, coral, all shades of pink, lilac, red, burgundy, royal blue, rainbow coloured and black.

**Orchid;** A timeless and exotic flower which can give a unique and tropical touch to your floral choices. Symbolising beauty, refinement, love and luxury, what's not to like? So delicate and grown in three variations; phalaenopsis, dendrobium and cymbidium. Mostly an autumn and winter flower and probably one of the more expensive flowers to purchase. Your colour choices are white, pink, red, green, purple, blue, orange and yellow. Some variations only flower in certain colours and not all of those choices.

**Jasmine;** With it's rich, exotic fragrance, it's a beautiful addition to your floral bouquet. These small delicate flowers symbolise purity, innocence, admiration and respect. And if your having a later wedding, you will enjoy their scent during this time as this is when it's mostly released. Jasmine is mostly white flowers, but sometimes certain varieties can produce yellow or pink flowers. Grown from spring to autumn.

**Tulips;** Mean perfect deep love. Tulips are a timeless, classic flower and a favourite for a wedding bouquet. Grown all year round, they are an accessible flower choice, too, coming in lots of colours such as white, cream, pink, red, orange, yellow, lilac, violet, purple and black. Some varieties are bicolour, too, where their petals are edged in a contrasting colour to the main flower. In fact, there are approximately 130 different options of tulips to choose from.

**Hydrangea;** The flower well known for its large voluptuous blooms, this flower can be enough on its own for a simple, lightweight, beautiful bouquet. Grown all year round. However, certain colours are only seasonal. Colours are blue, pink, purple, green, white, red, autumnal burgundy and yellow. Hydrangea represents gratitude, grace and beauty. They can be temperamental flowers with changes in humidity and must stay hydrated for as long as possible.

**Gardenia;** Considered to be a luxury wedding flower, offering brides an aesthetically pleasing and unique bouquet. Representing love, beauty and joy. They have a sweet fragrance and come in the colours red, pink, lemon and white. Perfect for a summer wedding.

**Daisy;** The flower that brings a sense of innocence, cheerfulness and happy mood to your wedding. Available from spring to autumn, this happy flower comes in white and yellow and symbolises loyalty, love and purity.

**Carnations;** The traditional wedding flower, it is one of the oldest known flowers that has been around since the Romans. Called the flower of God, it symbolises fascination, distinction and love. Grown all year round and can be grown as a single stem or as a spray of carnations. Carnations come in white, cream, lemon, yellow, orange, peach, mint, lilac, violet, purple, red, burgundy, pink, cerise and a two-tone coloured carnation with a stripy coloured petal, with lots of variations. Sweet smelling too.

**Sweet pea;** Signifying lasting pleasure. This flower has such sweet, delicate flower petals and has an amazing scent. Flowers in white, pink and purple with darker and lighter shades of each main block colour. If you are getting married in June or July, this could be a contender for you.

**Gerbera;** Part of the daisy family, they represent simple beauty and very happy life. Grown all year round, these happy flowers are a celebration of life. They come in lots of colours like white, cream, lemon, yellow, peach, orange, red, pink, and cerise and variations where the flower head has different types of petals on them, some spiky looking, some two-toned and even some that look like tagliatelle. Bringing joy in all shapes and sizes.

**Ranunculus;** Part of the buttercup family. This bloom has a lot of fine, delicate layers of petals similar to a peony, but the size of the flower is a lot smaller than that of a peony. Symbolising charm and attractiveness, this flower grows in cream, lemon, apricot, pink, orange, red and burgundy. Having no scent, it's perfect for people with allergies. It's a spring flower only.

**Freesia;** This sweet, fruity-scented flower is a popular one. Certain colours have a stronger scent than others, red, yellow and white being the strongest, and lilac and pink having a less potent scent. Meaning trust and friendship, this lovely intoxicating flower is available in Spring and Summer.

**Lily of the valley;** Part of the lily family, this particular flower represents happiness, purity, sincerity and innocence. Makes sense as it only flowers in white. Having a spring-like crisp, floral scent, slightly like jasmine. Also known as May bells, as that when it flowers, Spring.

**Lilac;** This spring time flower is a delicate, drapey and a bit of a romantic flower. Highly fragrant and symbolising love and innocence. Only flowers in white, pink and lilac. This romantic flower looks well on its own in a simple classic bouquet. Like a Hydrangea, it needs to be in the water and will wilt in the hot sunshine.

**Gypsophila;** Also known as babies breath. This all-year-round wedding flower is part of the carnation family. Symbolising everlasting love, it's a popular choice for a wedding flower. Grown in white or pink shades. It can be used as a filler for your bouquets or as a bunch by itself for that rustic feel.

**Dahlia;** The flower of the valley, symbolises beauty, commitment and kindness. This hardy flower grows from summer to autumn. With its luscious smell and varieties on flower heads ranging from Pom Pom flowers to spiky and ones full of petals that curl at the ends. They are a great flower choice for autumn weddings. The colours they come in are white, yellow, orange, pink, cerise, red, burgundy, lavender, purple, black, coral, bronze, and two-tone coloured dahlias are also available.

**Anemone;** Commonly called windflowers, there are roughly 120 species of anemones, and they have a wide variety of colours, white, purple, violet, blue, red, pink and yellow, all in lots of different shades of these colours. Originating from Japan, these beautiful flowers have paper-thin petals and come from the buttercup family. Symbolising forsaken love, these make a beautiful winter and spring flower.

**Sunflowers;** The happy flower symbolising loyalty and adoration. Their name comes from their unique behaviour to face the sun and follow the sun's radar, making them a great flower choice for a summer or autumn wedding. The petals appear in yellow, orange and red.

**Daffodils;** One of the first flowers to bloom in springtime, you know winter is over when you see these bloom, giving it the meaning of new beginnings. A spring flower that brings cheer and will flower in yellow or white.

**Lisianthus;** The flower of appreciation, charm and gratitude. Often mistaken for being part of the rose family. Grown all year round. This beautiful flower comes in white, green, yellow, peach, pink, lilac, purple, red, and rose colours. Some even are white with a different coloured tip.

**Lavender;** This strong-scented flower can come as a fresh flower or a dried flower, dried obviously being made all year round but fresh only being available from June to August. This purple flower represents devotion, grace, purity and serenity. Part of the mint family.

**Chrysanthemum;** Symbolising fidelity, joy and optimism. This flower has lots of varieties, some on a single stem, some as a spray, all with different shapes and sizes. Grown all year round for most of them, and they come in lots of different colours with lots of different shades in that colour white, cream, yellow, green, orange, pink, purple, red, autumnal, and stripy coloured.

**Protea;** Grown in South Africa and also known as the sugarbush. This large-headed flower is perfect for any tropical wedding bouquet, with its bold colours and textured shape. Symbolising diversity and courage, not surprising with its ability to change and transform as a flower. Flowers are mainly in Winter and Spring and come in pink, red, white, yellow and cream colours.

**Larkspur;** Also known as delphinium and a perfect flower for a whimsical, rustic wedding bouquet, with its delicate petals. Flowers in blue, pink, purple, red and white. Representing the strong bond of love. Available in the later parts of spring, summer and early autumn.

I hope this helps in your flower choices and what they represent for you in your bridal flowers. The foliage used in your bouquets also signifies some symbolic meaning too. Here are the most commonly used foliages in your bridal arrangements and what they symbolise.

**Ivy;** everlasting life and devotion
**Fern;** love and security
**Eucalyptus;** purifying and protection
**Olive;** peace
**Oak;** strength and stability
**Ruscus;** thoughtfulness

**Flowers to be wary of in your bouquets;**

The most well-known of all is the lily. As much as they smell divine, it can be overwhelming to some, and their pollen is a nightmare if it gets on your clothes. Other flowers with tricky pollen that stains your clothes are poppies.

Flowers that are temperamental with being too hot and wilting or need to be in the water a lot and do not last long outside of that are lilacs, hydrangeas, hellebores, astilbe and tulips.

Flowers that don't play nice with other flowers are daffodils, so unless you just have daffodils on their own, they with poison your other flowers.

Peonies bruise easily and are very delicate so just be careful with them. Good luck!

**Notes;**

# Colours and their meanings

## How do you choose your wedding colours?

The colours you choose for your wedding should represent you both. Take the time to find out what colour preferences you both have. What would you like your wedding to look like? What vision would you like your guests to see?

Your wedding day is a celebration, and your colour choice needs to reflect your whole theme. What atmosphere do you want to create for yourselves and your guests?

Take into account the season in which you are to marry in, the venue, its grounds, and the décor. Maybe you have a family tradition of colour themes, or maybe certain colours are used in your culture or religion.

Your wedding colours should also represent your personalities, what type of wedding you're having and what your relationship means to you both. There are so many different colours out there, and we are not all the same in our likes and dislikes. We don't all necessarily like the same colours, some colours might give off a morbid feel, whilst others give out a traditional feel. What are you trying to portray with your colour scheme?

Tell your story through your colour choice. It's your day. Ask yourself whether your colour scheme goes with the venue decor or does it clash. Do they complement each other? Is it welcoming and close to how you envisioned your wedding and what it looked like in your mind?

Different cultures will have different meanings for colours. For instance people in parts of Europe, white is considered the colour of purity, and that is why it is the most popular colour for weddings, but in China, the colour white means death, so the brides wear red. But let's delve into colours and what they interpret and mean for Europe!

**Red;**

Passion, love, desire, joy, excitement, boldness, power

Red is a bold colour and can look better as an accent instead of being your main colour. Red can ignite desire and make you more excited, pick up the romance with a vibrant red or tone it down with a beautiful burgundy. It is also a colour known for attracting money. Red and white say all the right things as two colours together. Types of red, maroon, scarlet, ruby, and crimson, to name a few.

Colour combinations: cherry red and black, burgundy and gold, cardinal red and grey, crimson and light brown, red and ivory.

**Pink;**

Romance, soft, sweet, feminine, caring.

Pink is a feminine colour and can come in lots of shades, fuchsia, rose, blush, magenta, and baby pink, just to name a few common shades used in weddings. Blush and navy weddings are a hot trend right now.

Colour combinations: dusky pink and ivory, light pink and navy, blush and mint, carnation and magenta, light pink and grey.

**Blue;**

Calm, peaceful, loyalty, reliability, serenity, spiritual.

Known for being a calming colour and a colour of trust. The "something blue" part of your wedding traditions stems from the belief that blue symbolises love, fidelity and trust. There are lots of ways you can carry on this tradition if you want something blue as part of your wedding colour scheme, blue heels, and blue sashes, to name a couple. Don't forget shades like turquoise, teal, cobalt, peacock, sapphire, navy, and indigo, to name a few.

Blue is also a colour that can be used in winter weddings, pairing light blue with silver, think Disney's Frozen, with sparkly snowflakes everywhere.

Colour combinations: navy and cranberry, pale blue and ivory, cerulean and sage, pale blue and gold, navy and ivory, light blue and yellow.

**Purple;**

Royalty, luxury, power, elegance, spiritual

A popular colour choice for couples. Purple was associated with wealth and opulence and was traditionally exclusively worn by nobility and royalty. Darker shades of purple signify luxury and power, whilst lighter shades of purple give off a sense of elegance, magic and a whimsical affair. With shades like violet, lilac, periwinkle and lavender, mauve, mulberry, plum, aubergine and grape, there are lots of shades to go from with this colour. It's also known for attracting money.

Purple is a colour scheme that can be used at any time of the year. For winter, if you pair darker shades of purple with gold, it will give a glamorous feel to your wedding. Or pair a lighter shade of purple with ivory or sage; it will give off a romantic, whimsical feel perfect for your springtime weddings. Purple flowers are also quite beautiful.

Colour combinations; lilac and sage, plum and gold, dark purple and light grey, lavender and yellow, lilac and ivory.

## Orange;

Warmth, cheerfulness, excitement, vitality, youth

A difficult colour to pull off in winter but perfect for spring blooms, summer vibes and autumn rustic feels. If you're going for a boho vibe, this colour comes together with burnt orange, dusky pink and browns. Shades to look out for are coral, tangerine, apricot, peach, bronze, rust and amber; there are so many shades of this colour. It's a fun colour.

Perfect colour for autumnal, rustic weddings teamed with browns, greens, and yellows. Dried florals teamed with darker shades of orange will give off an earthy feel to your wedding, and pumpkin and Halloween weddings are a must with orange.

Colour combinations: tangerine and yellow, orange, cranberry and yellow, apricot and sage, orange, teal and gold, peach, ivory and dusky pink.

## Yellow;

Happiness, positivity, optimistic, joy, awareness

Yellow just screams energy and happiness. And for couples who are creative and enjoy learning and exploring, yellow also signifies curiosity and imagination. Gold is a good choice as it traditionally represented prosperity and riches. Having yellow flowers in your bouquet brings hope and enlightenment.

Primarily associated with spring and summer weddings, with brighter shades of yellow, but if you adopt a more golden tone for autumn weddings, this will bring a warm feel to your wedding.

Shades, canary, lemon, bumblebee, pineapple, gold and corn are a few of them.

Colour combinations: canary and light blue, yellow and coral, emerald, cream and gold, yellow and lilac, yellow, mint and ivory, lemon, cream and navy.


## Green;

Harmony, growth, fertility, health, nature, calm, bounty

Often used by brides to signify their love of nature and the outdoors, you can do this by using brighter shades of green. As green is also associated with wealth and money, if you want to bring this into your theme, choose darker rich shades of green. It has a deep emotional analogy with the feelings of being secure.

If you are going for a nature-inspired wedding, take full advantage of the natural foliage available to you in your wedding decor. Drape garlands, hang foliage, and use it to your advantage.

Shades of green, mint, lime, pistachio, sage, forest, hunter, British racing and emerald are a few for you.

Colour combinations: emerald and gold, sage and blush pink, mint, light blue and ivory, olive and ivory, sage, dusky pink and navy, lime, navy and cobalt.


## Brown;

Earthiness, steadfast, dependable, health, simplicity

For your rustic, vintage, barn-style weddings, brown hues bring it all altogether. Whether it's the hessian or burlap as your sashes, wood stumps for name tags or wooden crates with flowers in and around your venue.

Brown is one of the easiest wedding colours for brides for these types of vibes. You can really bring the rustic element alive with brown. Great colour for any season, with your autumnal shades teamed with brown, your tweed suits for summer weddings, your gingerbread and hot chocolates for winter and dried floral features for spring, it's a good all-rounder.

Shades like mocha, mink, caramel, gingerbread, pecan, brunette and chocolate and more for brown lovers.

Colour combinations: peanut, sage and tortilla, brunette, hunter and orange, dusky pink, sage and tortilla, mink, dusky pink and ivory.

## White;

Innocence, purity, peace, simplicity, kindness, newness

In ancient times brides wore a white tunic on their wedding day, representing their purity and symbolising both the woman's chastity and her transition to being a married woman. Fast forward to today, and most brides have some shade of white in their wedding arrangements. Whether it's their dress, their flowers, or their cake, it will more than likely be somewhere.

The colour is an all-year rounder and goes with almost every other colour or shade there is, whether you are having a winter wedding with snowy features, a bright yellow and white spring affair, or a beach summer wedding in bright whites. Shades of white are in most brides' wedding themes.

Shades of white, ivory, cream, pearl, porcelain, linen, lace, and chiffon, to name but a few.

Colour combinations: dusky pink, ivory and sage, navy and lace, light grey, chiffon and royal blue, white and red, white and yellow.

## Black;

Sexy, sophisticated, strength, power, elegant

Black can symbolise the power of love when worn at a wedding, whether it's a black ring, black suit, or black sash on a chair. It shows that you are dedicated to your marriage and that you believe in the strength of your union above all else. Black can add chic and glamour to your wedding with either a touch here and there with a sprinkle of black, or you could go for nothing but dark details. It's up to you guys.

Going for glam, have an all-white cake with a black cake topper.

Start off on the right foot with a black monogram on your aisle runner.

Welcome your guests with a black welcome sign; feeling rustic, use a blackboard.

So much you can involve black in at your wedding.

Thinking there is only one shade of black, think again, ink, ebony, jet black, coal, leather and charcoal, to name a few.

Colour combinations: black, emerald and gold, onyx and white. Ink and red, black, pink and ivory, charcoal, silver and lace.

**Grey;**

Modesty, neutral, balance,

The colour between black and white literally means without colour; it's neutral. This neutral colour is perfect for any season as it pairs perfectly with so many other colours. There is nothing dull or gloomy about this colour at a wedding. Pair it well, and it will bring the perfect tone to your day. A grey wedding is sophisticated.

Over a hundred shades of grey, actually, with pewter, silver, slate, dove, and porpoise being some of them.

Colour combinations: peach and light grey, dusky pink, sage and slate, emerald, pewter and ivory, cerise, dark grey and lace.

## Pastel shades;

Pastel colours are lighter shades of your main block colour. Generally considered to be feminine and delicate.

These shades are considered to soothe and bring peace. Great for whimsical springtime weddings or beach vibes at a summer wedding.

These lighter, buttery shades bring warmth and hope and will grab the attention of everyone at your wedding.

## Bold shades;

Making a more striking appearance, these colours are bright and energetic and bring the pop to enhance the personality of your wedding.

Vibrant colours are perfect for anyone wanting to give their wedding some extra sparkle.

Just be careful you don't clash with certain colours, that's all.

Have fun! This is a great time in your wedding planning stages, and your wedding is coming together once you have your colour scheme. Most of your other plans will fit in once this has been decided.

**Notes;**

# Music and other entertainment

The music/songs you will need for your wedding are as follows;

- Something to walk down the aisle to
- 2 songs for signing of the register
- Something to walk out of the ceremony to
- Reception drinks, music
- Background music for your wedding breakfast
- First dance song
- Evening reception music

## Ceremony music:

If your having a civil ceremony, you possibly won't be allowed to use overly religious music. And if your having a church ceremony, there will be limits as to what kind of music you're allowed for your ceremony too. Either way, if you check with your church or venue what the limits are so, you can find the perfect wedding ceremony music that will be allowed and given the go-ahead.

Make the music appropriate for yourselves, your venue and your ceremony type. Set the mood, and your wedding day will be emotional and romantic. Enhance all these magical feelings with your ceremony music.

You could always personalise your ceremony music by one of you choosing the walking down the aisle music and the other person choosing the walking out of ceremony music, choose a song that represents the way you feel about each other, something that you know the other person would appreciate, or be thrilled to hear, maybe even one that holds a special memory for you both. Keep it a surprise till the day for extra romance.


**Reception music;**

Just after your ceremony, you may want to keep the music more ambient and comfortable for everyone whilst you mingle and talk to people. Consider the volume of your music, so people are not shouting over the music. Maybe choosing something calmer at this point whilst everyone chatters is more appropriate.

Whilst it may be appropriate to play light jazz or have a pianist playing at your reception drinks, they are not your only options; here are a few others for you to consider;

- other musicians like harpists, violinists, cellists, and a string quartet.
- a soul choir/band
- acoustic artists can make a great soundtrack whilst you mingle with your guests
- maybe a family friend can play or sing a few songs at your reception drinks
- record a playlist on a device that can be played on your venues sound system

Don't feel like you need to stay traditional at this point, have music that represents you both. Try not to make any rash decisions that you may regret, though. Maybe avoid overly negative songs or non-romantic songs with staying true to your tastes, though musicians can do their own takes on the likes of Ed Sheeran songs, for instance.

Live musicians can change the mood of the room as, and when it's needed, they can bring and air of elegance and sophistication to your wedding.

**First dance;**

When choosing your first dance, whether it's Ellie Goulding or Ella Henderson, you may want some inspiration.

Choose something sentimental to you both and signifies both of your personalities.

Listen to your music libraries, and get some lists going of songs you both like.

Ask your friends and family for their input. Maybe they can recommend their first dance song or a song suggestion of their own.

If you have a favourite celebrity, maybe use the first dance song that they had at their wedding.

Maybe your venue will inspire your choice of song.

Maybe you want your first dance to be a spectacle, and you'd rather it be the dance you want to embrace rather than the song choice, a quick waltz or a fiery tango? Or a choreographed pop number, whether it's both of you dancing together or one of you dancing for the other person. This is probably the newest trend of late. You could even take dance lessons to wow your partner and guests with your new dancing feet.

If you're a singer, why not serenade your partner with a song instead of a dance, whether you sing something that you know they will like or something to express your love for your partner? What a memory that would be. For you and your guests.

The tradition of the first dance is for you both to start the dancing off. Then traditionally, the dancing formations go off into this;

- Groom and his mother
- Bride and her father
- Then both parents dance together
- Groomsmen dance with the bridesmaids
- Groomsmen take turns dancing with the bride
- Bridesmaids take turns dancing with the groom
- Free for all

Get whisked off your feet however you choose to mark this tradition.


**Evening reception music;**

There is nothing you will appreciate more so at your evening reception than a packed dance floor. So getting the music right will determine if this happens or not. Do you have a live band? Or a DJ? And how do you make sure that all your favourite songs are played? A DJ will be able to provide you with a breadth of music choices, while a band can offer a more lively, interactive experience for you and your guests.

Your budget will determine if you have a live band or a DJ, and also your venue; they may have restrictions on live bands, so best to check with them first on that.

Ask your friends and family for referrals on a live band and a decent DJ. You could also ask your wedding co-ordinator from your wedding venue who they recommend. Check out social media sites for any recommendations for that area, especially if you are marrying out of town and you don't know the area at all. Your local wedding fair may have some resources too. Hopefully, musicians will be in attendance so you can hear what they are like first-hand.

Questions to ask your perspective band or DJ
- How many breaks do you take and for how long
- Is pre-recorded music played whilst the break is on
- What are their overtime policies and rates of pay if you guys run over
- Is there a backup plan in place in the event of a problem
- Is there back up equipment or instruments if a problem occurs with these

Make sure all of these answers are in their contract

Don't sign anything without either watching a performance on video or in person

Take note of their sound quality, performance style and their appearance. If you don't like what you see, move onto the next option

Read the reviews, and if you see any complaints along the lines of tacky outfits, corny jokes, or talking too much, you should probably keep looking.

Once you've booked your band or DJ, start getting your music together. Do you want an entrance song? Or a last dance song? You need to be looking at around 15 songs per hour, and a typical wedding would probably have around 3 hours of dancing after the wedding breakfast, which makes 45 songs.

Maybe you want to start your evening off with your favourite tunes from the 80s, whatever you want to do, but you do want to be selecting meaningful music for you both to enjoy, give your band or DJ a list of songs you want to be played and when, for instance, the walking in and out songs, first dance etc., or if easier give them a "don't play" list for your music, so you don't have to listen to any songs you don't like.

Things you could also do to choose your music;

- Check out the DJ's most requested wedding songs
- Have a look at your favourite singers or bands for songs you like
- Ask your guests for suggestions on their invites for songs
- Make your playlist shareable for guests
- Listen to the list of songs once you've got it together, and make sure you like it
- Add a mix of genres
- Try to include at least 1 slow song for every 5 fast songs

Have fun creating, and keep the downloads so you can listen to them in years to come.

**Alternative entertainment;**

What can you do if you are not a keen dancer, or you don't want music at your reception, and you want to provide something different to the norm? Some can be so much fun that your guests won't even notice there's no dancing on the dance floor.

Outdoor wedding,
- Lawn games, croquet, tin can alley, hook a duck, coconut shy, hoopla, and bullseye, to name a few

- Treasure hunt

- Take your music/band/DJ outdoors, like a mini-concert

- Clay pigeon shooting

- Archery

- Target shooting, cork shooting alley

- Ball games, roll a ball, ball in a bucket

Maybe you could utilise some of these games for your guests whilst you are off having your romantic photographs of just the two of you, so they are entertained.

Other alternatives that can suit indoor or outdoor weddings;

- Good ol' board games

- Murder mystery to solve between yourselves

- Pop quiz, hold your very own year of marriage quiz

- Bingo session, with prizes, like a raffle

- Tarot card reader

- Magician or illusionist

- Vegas-inspired dancers

- Drag performance

- Stand-up comedian

- Live painter or caricature artist

- Interactive champagne servers

- Burlesque show, can-can dancers

Go with your theme, go with what it means to you both, and what overall feel do you want to achieve? Whatever you decide, be happy with the decisions you've made.

**Notes;**

**Cars and transport;**

Depending on your choices for your wedding so far, some of you may not need wedding cars. For instance, if you are holding your ceremony in the same venue as your wedding reception, there would be no need for a wedding car.

If your ceremony venue/church is somewhere different to your wedding reception venue, then you would need to consider wedding cars for yourselves and possibly for your guests. If you want to provide transport for your guests, that is.

**Who goes in a wedding car?**

The size of your wedding party will determine if you need 1 or 2 wedding cars, usually wedding cars seat between 3 and 6 passengers, and some firms will make a certain amount of trips included in their price, depending on how many people you have to go in cars and how far away your venue actually is from your collection point, will determine how many wedding cars you will actually need. Traditionally though;

The bride travels with her father or the person who is giving her away in one car.

The bridesmaids and the bride's mother, and the flower girls will go in another car.

The groom will usually go with the best men and ushers, and not necessarily in a wedding car, again depending on your budget, maybe a luxury speed car, a hummer to fit everyone in, the best man's car, or for the daredevils there is even a helicopter or speed boat depending on where your venue is, nothing is to be ruled out when it comes to the men.

The wedding cars will pick you up from your collection point and then take you to your church or venue. Then if you are going on somewhere else, like a different venue, they will take your bridal party there. This is where you may need more than 1 car. As usually, you would both go off together to have your private wedding photos done with your photographer, so you may have to take this into consideration during your planning stages if this is the case.

Wedding car hire firms will also set an amount of time in their costs too. Most firms allow 3 hours for all trips. You may want to find out if they charge an extension fee should you run over time; you never know.

Your wedding cars will come with chauffeur drivers.


**What choices of cars or other transport?**

Cars for you and your bridal party, lots of different styles to choose from, here are a few ideas;


Traditional;
Mercedes, Rolls-Royce, Bentley, Jaguar, BMW, Aston Martin, Audi


Vintage;
vintage Chevrolet, vintage Beauford, vintage Rolls-Royce, vintage Regent,


Quirky;
VW camper van, VW beetle, Cadillac, flatbed truck, taxi,


Larger parties;
Vintage bus, Hummer, Limousine, Hummer Limousine,

Boys and their cars;

Lamborghini, the A team van, Bond car, Dukes of Hazzard car,

Car alternatives;

Horse and carriage, bicycle, Vespa, boat, helicopter, tractor, skateboard

Take into account your venue and its distance away from where you will be getting ready.

How many is the transport for?

Are you transporting your guests to your venue?

Are you going off for photos elsewhere?

How many cars will you need?

## Car decorations;

Tins, cans, and shoes tied on the back of cars with white ribbons were all used traditionally to symbolise a married couple newly married and ward off evil spirits that may harm them.

Fast forward to today, and your wedding cars are still decorated with ribbons. Some companies will use ribbons in your colour scheme to match up. However, a lot will use white or ivory to keep it traditional.

To decorate your getaway car once your hitched, traditionally, it would be the responsibility of your bridal party, more so the groomsmen, really. However, you could leave it to your wedding planner or even yourself. A great photo opportunity and one not to be missed.

However, if you don't fancy the tin cans and shoes, here are a few ideas that you could decorate your car with;

: Flower garland

: Large fabric tassels

: Balloons

: Floral wreath

: Bright ribbons and bright flowers

: Foliage garland

: Fabric sign

**Notes;**

# Venue decor

Styling your venue will primarily depend on what type of wedding you're having and what venue you have it in. If, for instance, you're having a tipi wedding, you may need to source everything from your tables, chairs, and toilet facilities to your table decorations, seating areas and dancing area. If you are holding all of your weddings in the same venue, it may include a lot of venue decor within the wedding package price.

The first thing and best thing to do is to check your contract. If you have signed it already before checking, see what is included in your package price with your wedding handler, whether that's the venue itself, your wedding planner, or any hire company. The venue may only include the bare essentials like your table and chairs, linens etc. Your wedding planner should advise you of what's included in any of your packages. Check the small print with everything and everyone you book for your wedding. You don't want to be caught out on your wedding day.

### What does venue decor consist of?

### : Tables and chairs

Depending on your venue, you will either need to hire these from an events furniture hire company, in which you will be able to choose the type of chair you want and the style of table. Maybe you want picnic benches instead of formal-style tables.

Or you will get tables and chairs included in your venue package. Depending on your venue, some of them have conference-style chairs that may not necessarily go with your wedding theme or colour scheme, so you may want to cover these with a chair cover and a pretty bow that will go with your wedding theme and colour scheme. Unless included in your venue package, for this, you would need a venue stylist. They will be able to provide you with chair covers and bow sashes for your chairs.

Chair covers range from colours, white and ivory being your more commonly used colours, but you can also get them in black too. They come in a stretchy lycra chair cover which is fitted to the chair or a loose linen chair cover.

Chair bows come in a lot of different materials and colours, such as organza, satin, lace, taffeta, chiffon, and sequins. They can come in plain block colours or patterns. A venue stylist will be able to go through this in more depth for you, maybe you want to match your colour scheme, or maybe you want to pull out a different colour altogether. Your choice.

Some venues may have the new modern style of chair called the Chiavari chairs. These may come in a lime wash, white, gold or acrylic style. You will either like them on their own or with a chair bow just to give it something else, and your venue stylist will be able to help you with this.

Some brides will even go with more chair accessory dressing and may want to put something in the back of the chair bow to give it that something extra. This could be a flower, a bit of foliage or a brooch.


### : Table linen and napkins

If you have to hire your tables for your wedding reception, the table you choose may not need a tablecloth. For instance, picnic tables are probably not going to need a tablecloth. If you do need to hire tablecloths, make sure you know the size of your table so you can get the right-sized cover, table cloths are usually white or ivory, but some linen hires companies will do different coloured tablecloths. You will also be able to hire napkins from a linen company or a catering company if you have to hire caterers too. You might be able to hire different coloured napkins to match your colour scheme; if not, it's white or ivory.

If your venue provides tablecloths and napkins as part of their package, these will probably be in either white or ivory unless the venue can provide any other colour. Venues tend to arrange your napkins in a certain arranged display too, for instance, a napkin arranged like a flower or a fan.

Venue stylists and linen hire companies have table overlays that you can hire to dress up your tables differently if you want something more than a plain tablecloth, overlays in lace, sequins, florals, and different colours.

Napkin dressing can come in the form of a flower on each napkin, which your florist can arrange for you. Or maybe a ribbon tie around your napkin that matches your colour scheme. You could do a tie ribbon for a man and a bow for a lady. This would usually be done by whoever does your place settings, like a stationary person.

## : Crockery and cutlery

If you have to hire caterers for your wedding reception, they should provide the crockery and cutlery needed for your reception.

If you're having a vintage-style wedding, you will be able to hire vintage-style crockery and cutlery from a vintage decor hire firm. They will also hire teapots, coffee pots, sugar bowls, teacups and saucers, and even cake stands for your sandwich triangles.

If you are having your wedding reception in a venue that is providing you with your meal arrangements, they will provide you with the crockery and cutlery required in your package.

If you have food trucks or outdoor food vendors, they should provide you with utensils to eat and be merry.

**: Drinks glasses**

Your wedding venue will provide these if they are providing you with your catering; they will usually supply you with a wine glass for the meal, a champagne glass for the toast, and a tumbler for any water for each guest.

If you are hiring caterers to supply your food, you should be able to hire glasses from them for you and your guests, some may only hire plastic glasses, and you may want to double up on your glass usage, for instance, if you are supplying wine as a toast and as part of the meal, you may only need to hire 1 wine glass per person. If your caterer does not supply glassware, then there are glassware companies out there that do.

Another option is if you are hiring out a bar service, prosecco wall or van, cocktail van or drinks vendors, they may be able to hire drinks glasses for you.

Vintage wedding? The vintage decor hire firms will be able to hire decanters for your tables, maybe even crystal glasses for you and your guests.

**: Aisle runner or carpet**

A wedding venue may provide you with an aisle carpet for your ceremony. Best to check if it's red or ivory first. And also, check if it's included in your package or is a chargeable extra.

Venue stylists can hire out aisle carpets for certain other wedding venues that don't provide them or other types of weddings. It would be down to the suppliers' discretion if they hire it out to you for, say, an outdoor wedding.

If you don't fancy an aisle carpet, maybe do something different, like a petal aisle, and walk on crushed flowers (maybe only with an outdoor wedding).

What about a monogram aisle runner customised for you both?

### : Material swagging for your ceremony tables

A wedding venue may include some table swagging in your package. If not, the swagging would be done by a venue stylist and charged for in addition. A venue stylist would also swag your tables if you were having your wedding elsewhere too.

Ceremony tables that could have additional material swag on them would be;

Registrar table, top table, cake table, gift table.

The material swagging is in either an organza, chiffon or satin material. You can usually get it to match the colour of your chair bows and other decors.

The swagging just frames your tables and gives them some depth.

### : Floral decor on your registrar table, top table and guest tables

Unless your wedding venue includes any of these arrangements in their wedding packages, these arrangements would be arranged with either your florist or venue stylist.

Floral arrangements on your registrar table should go with your wedding theme and colour scheme. This arrangement could be a traditional piece which is a long and low arrangement that sits on the table in front of you both, or maybe you want a whimsical, dreamy arrangement which overflows your table. Some people don't want flowers and will opt for a modern candle display, varying in height for visual effect.

Usually, what you choose to have on your registrar table will be moved over onto your top table by the venue stylist or wedding staff at your venue. If your top table is a long table with more guests on it, then you may want to extend your arrangement to fill the whole top table. Either that or you keep your original piece to just sit in front of you both to frame yourselves. Some couples choose to have their new married names in a carving in front of themselves, for instance, Mr and Mrs Harvey.

Your guest tables tend to have some sort of arrangement in the middle of their table. This ideally needs to flow with your colour scheme, wedding theme and your other arrangements that are on your top table, whether that's a floral arrangement or candle display. Your venue stylist should be able to guide you into their recommendations that match everything. Table arrangements could be displayed in a vase, tall or short. Maybe you have a blossom theme, and you want blossom trees as your centrepieces on your guest tables. Or an autumn theme where your decorations are pumpkin arrangements. Once you have your theme and colour scheme, this will all flow together.

Florist and venue stylist is key on this point.


**: Petals, lanterns or other aisle decorations**

Imagine walking down the aisle. Do you envisage walking down to candlelight, glowing in the romantic light, with petals strewn on the floor? Maybe you want to walk under a canopy of trees or flowers in a midsummer's night dream.

Your aisle chairs could be dressed on the side of the chair with beautiful bows or chair florals so you pass them as you walk down the aisle.

Whether your wedding ceremony is indoors or outdoors, your aisle decor can be arranged with your venue stylist.

**: Archways/trees or other decors for your ceremony room**

Depending on your venue and the features it has in the room, you may want to decorate it, or you may not. Maybe it's a blank canvas, and the more you decorate, the better, or maybe your venue has features, and not a lot of things need to be added to it for it to be perfect.

An outdoor wedding in its natural setting, will it need anything more?

A venue stylist will advise you if the venue or space you have needs anything else in terms of decor.

An archway could be set up so you walk under it to meet your soon-to-be spouse, or you could marry under an archway. Imagine a postcard picture of you both under the arch. There are many various shapes and sizes of archways, floral archways, foliage archways, balloon archways, material drape arches, pampas archways and a mix of them all archways. A moon-shaped arch, a heart shape, hexagon archways, and rectangular framed arches. Choose them in your colour scheme, so everything flows.

Other decors that could be achieved in a venue if it has a medieval chandelier light fitting that could have florals draped down off it for extra effect. Wall sconces with foliage dropped down off them. Fireplace dressing, window displays, entrance door displays, there is such a lot you could decorate if you wanted to and your venue allowed you to. Always best to check with your venue what you are allowed to dress and what you are not allowed to dress. They may have restrictions.

Outdoor tipis, marquees and other outdoor venues may be the same. Always best to check first.

Especially before any money has changed hands.


### : Ceiling drapes or ceiling lights

Depending on your venue, as some venues may already provide this extra detail, but for those venues or places where you may want to add some extra features to your wedding decor, ceiling drapes can add a certain spectacle to your room or area. They would usually come in a white or ivory chiffon-type material and maybe drape up and over certain features in your venue's ceiling area.

Ceiling lights can give your room a certain feel, especially if they are colour-coordinated to your colour scheme. They would give your room just that something extra, especially if it's quite a dark room with dark features. Lights will lift it a bit; twinkly fairy lights displayed over certain features within the ceiling area can give off a romantic, homely feeling too.

Other decor you could use in the ceiling area is foliage. Maybe your venue has beams on show. Maybe wrapping the beams in ivy and having it trailing down from the beams will give off a romantic vibe, with vines twisting around together like 2 lovers. Simple but very effective.

Your venue stylist should be able to help guide you with any of these features.


### : Additional lighting like up lighters

These would be your alternative lighting for you to give your area or rooms that extra lighting. These would usually be a part of a DJ's equipment so they can light up the area around where they will be working to give the area a more disco feel. Some up-lighters are colour-coordinated to your colour scheme. Some of them will give off a warm glow, and some of them will be multi-coloured to give off that happy, let's dance feeling.

If a DJ doesn't have these as part of their equipment, then either your venue will. If they don't, then you would have to look at a lighting company that would hire them for you.

### : Love letters and signs

These large signs come in various words, sizes and styles. Depending on the word, they can be displayed in the area you are having your ceremony, on their own and then moved to your reception area, or just be in your wedding breakfast room, which will then go into your evening reception area.

The signs usually start from 3ft in height, going up to about 6ft in height, and they tend to have lights fitted into the words, so they light up, it's a great feature to have at your wedding, and you can get some awesome pictures featuring the lights in with you and your guests.

They usually come in large white letters or rustic wooden letters. The words you can make are; love, I do, dance, party, Mr & Mrs, Mr & Mr, Mrs & Mrs, and then your surname to follow, both of your initials, disco.

Alternative to the large free-standing signs, you have neon signs. Usually, they need to be attached to an archway frame or a backing board of some kind, like a floral board or foliage board, and these can come in lots of colours and wording. If you have them personalised by a company, then obviously, you could get your new married name on a neon sign. However, if you choose a company that you can just hire the sign off of them, they tend to be just certain wordings like; happily ever after, better together, love wins, all you need is love, the drinks are on us, crazy in love, all of me loves all of you, drunk in love, it was always you.

Alternatives to light-up signs, you could use floral letters or signs, possibly smaller in size than the light-up signs but just as effective. You could use a signpost with several arrows with words coming off the post, and you could even do this yourself if you wanted, telling guests it's this way to the dancing, this way to the bar, this way to where we say I do, that kind of thing.

The vintage or large mirror stood up on an easel with information or wordings on for your guests. You could do the same with a blackboard and a frame easel.

Venue stylists may stock some of these features, and lighting equipment hire firms. Some DJs may even have certain items that they can hire out to you if you book them as your DJ.

## : Place settings and names for your guests

These can come in various forms, and unless you have a wedding reception where people can sit anywhere and it's very informal, your guests will need to know where they are sitting. So each guest will need a place card or something with their name on the table at their place setting.

If you've hired a stationer to do your invites, order of service and other stationery items, they could match your place cards to the items you've produced before. Stationers will either be able to print your place cards or use calligraphy writing on your cards for that more personal touch. They can be produced on cards, name tags, wooden plaques, and acrylic plaques.

You could set the scene on your tables at their place setting; there would be their name, their wedding favour, maybe a bit of foliage or a flower, maybe their place card is set into a mini log to hold it in place, or it's tied with a cute piece of ribbon.

If you don't want to hire a stationer, maybe this is something you could do together or with your bridesmaids.

### : Seating settings

These can also be done in various forms as well, and again unless you're having a free for all where people can sit where ever they want to sit, your guests will need to see and be directed to which table they are sitting on.

If you've hired a stationer, this can match the theme that you've set out on your invitations, order of service and place cards etc. this item would be called a table plan. These can be printed on a board and placed on an easel at the entrance to your wedding reception. Easels would normally be provided by your wedding venue or the stationery person you've hired.

Other ways of producing your table plan; include calligraphy writing on a board or mirror on an easel. Printed or handwritten tags pegged on a string board, picture frame or wooden crate. Painted table plans on a wooden pallet, table plan cards hung off a wishing tree, table plans on an acrylic board, table plan cards in picture frames, placed sporadically on vintage ladders or a vintage sideboard, table plans hung off an archway frame instead of an easel. If you are feeling very creative, what about individual pictures of your guests, like a polaroid picture pegged up on a picture frame or string board?

Your stationer will be able to advise you and create something for you both that matches your theme. Or do it between yourselves. Get the bridesmaids involved.

### : Gift and guest area

This area is usually where your guests will leave your gifts, where your guests will sign your guest book, and it's usually where you will put a memory acknowledgement for any loved ones that are not in attendance at your wedding. This is usually all arranged on a dressed table; if you are at a venue, this should be included in your package and should be arranged for you by their wedding coordinator. They should also put your items out and display them for you on the table. If you are not in a venue and you want to arrange something like this in a certain area, maybe get one of your bridal parties to arrange your items in a certain place or area for you. You ideally don't want to be doing any of this on your wedding day.

Gift area;

You are more than likely going to receive cards on your wedding day, and you are going to want to store these somewhere safe during your day. Some venues may provide a post box of sorts in their wedding packages, and most people will need to organise their own. Your stationer will have things you can hire from them, like a postbox, a card suitcase, a glasshouse for cards, and a wishing well. Just make sure they are lockable, so your gifts are secure.

Guest book;

Getting your guests to sign their name, write a message to you both, and write a funny or memorable quote or something for you to look back on in years to come is a task in itself, and it would make great sense if you could give this task to an usher, best-man or someone from your bridal party to go round the guests to get this done, as people forget and before you know it nothing has been signed and you end up with an empty book. A guest book is the traditional option and can be decorated by your stationery to match your other stationery items. Other options for guests to sign something would be; a picture frame of you both and your guests signing around the edge of your picture. This is a good one just so you can frame the picture and hang it at home and have a constant reminder of your day. Get your guests to sign pieces of a jigsaw, so when you put it together at home, you can see what your guests wrote. Guests can sign a wooden heart, and it then goes into a clear acrylic holder in a heart shape. Signatures and messages on a globe. Get your guests to write messages to go into a bottle. Whatever you decide to do, make sure your pens are all the same colour, there is nothing worse than everything being signed in one colour, and some guest has opted for a different colour, so it doesn't match at all.

Memory area;

This could be a poem you've made or printed yourself. You could frame this and put it alongside pictures of your loved ones that are no longer present. You could have a candle lit in memory of your loved ones. There are also frames or a box frame with a poem on it with feathers inside. You could display these on your gift table or have a solo area for this in commemoration, surround it with jars of flowers, candles, petals, or something peaceful. As long as it means something to you both, that's all that matters.

### : Dance floor area

There will be an area for dancing, whether it's a purpose-built dance floor or an area where you can dance, maybe on a flat floor or grassy area wherever you are having your wedding reception.

If you want a sparkly led, lighted dance floor to dance on and your venue doesn't provide you with one of these, you can usually hire them from your DJ or venue stylist. These are mostly additional extras. If you're lucky, they may be within your package price. They are simply lovely to dance the night away on.

### : Backdrops

These can come in various styles, designs and sizes. Usually, not part of any wedding package at a venue and will be charged as an additional extra.

It can be supplied by a venue stylist. They can be arranged in various ways around your wedding, some having them on a certain wall to get married in front of, making it a feature area, then when their room gets changed around from the ceremony room to the reception, their top table is placed in front of the backdrop so it's all framed nicely so you both can sit in front of a backdrop and it will provide great photos of you both. Some couples opt for a backdrop that is situated in their room so everyone can have photos in front of it. Some of them maybe frame their cake area. It's a great addition to your wedding, providing beautiful photo opportunities for you and your guests. A useful prop to have if there is anything you don't like about your venue, you can probably cover it up with your backdrop.

Starlight backdrops are probably your largest backdrops. They are approximately the length of a top table that seats 6/8 people and can go upwards of 7/8ft tall. They are an led lit up ivory or white curtain on a frame that is adjustable in height and length.

Other alternative backdrops, foliage backdrops may be staged with a neon sign, floral backdrops come in various colours and different flower choices, shimmer backdrops that will light up the way, you also have frames with ribbons attached or macrame, making a whimsical romantic rustic feel to your wedding. All giving you beautiful photographic memories of your wedding.


## : Balloons

An additional extra to your wedding tends to be extra decoration for your evening reception. Some couples have these as centrepieces for their guest tables, and some couples have them around their room as decoration. It can be colour-coordinated to your colour scheme.

Balloon staggers are a stagger of balloons in your colour scheme and usually come in sets of 3, 5, 7 and more, depending on your choice. Used as table decor or room decor.

Novelty balloons, the funny side of life in a balloon, maybe a giant bride, a giant ring, a giant church balloon, extra decor for the party at night time. Give them away as gifts for children at the end of the night.

Light up led balloons to give your evening reception that extra light, a bit of bling in a balloon.

You can also get balloons attached to an arch for that dramatic effect. You can colour-coordinate them to your scheme, maybe even with a sign on the frame, too, like a neon sign or something.

Balloon boxes are a new thing; you can get stacker boxes that spell Mr and Mrs or Mr and Mr, they are clear on the outside, and you can fill them with balloons on the inside, a different style of balloon decor for your wedding.

You can also get things to attach to the tails of your balloon, so rather than just having the ribbon on its own, you could have foliage trails off your balloon for extra effect, dangling ribbon tails, a tulle material tail, a floral tail, tassels, it just gives that something else to your balloon decor.

Give your balloons to guests as gifts at the end of your wedding, and maybe thank someone for their input on your day. That way, you don't have to take so many balloons home with you after the wedding.


### : Table settings

These are the extra little things that can go on your tables for your guests. Through your stationer, you could put menus on the tables, so people will remember what they have chosen to eat. If not an option, maybe put on the back of their place card what they ordered individually, helping the waitresses out serving too. You could name your tables instead of the traditional table 1, table 2. You could name your tables something that symbolises you both, like your favourite holiday destinations that you've taken together, your favourite bands, or your favourite chocolate bars. Honestly, it takes all sorts naming tables, just be true to yourselves and match your theme.

Additional crockery for your table, could insist on a charger plate, bring some colour to your table of white plates. Also, your venue or caterer will know how many plates and how much cutlery is required for each table setting, depending on how formal or informal your wedding meal is.

Bubbles for your guests to blow on for effective background pictures and additional fun.

Disposable cameras were always on everyone's tables at weddings, of old, they are handy to get your guests to capture moments that you wouldn't necessarily see yourselves on your wedding day.

Activity packs for children to keep them entertained.

Don't forget your wedding favours and place cards.

**Notes;**

# Wedding themes

## Do you need a theme?

In a word, yes, a wedding theme gives you something to work on, somewhere to start with your wedding preparations, it helps you make the decisions needed for your colour scheme and your wedding decor, and it helps keep your wedding uniform and not chaotic.

If you are confused over some decor ideas, or you are thinking of doing some or all of your wedding DIY, ask yourself, "is it something that fits with my wedding theme?" It's a great question to ask yourself when you don't know what to choose.

Your wedding theme is essentially the style of your wedding and how you want it to feel how you want it to look on your big day. What are you trying to emulate?

When you are choosing your wedding theme, consider these;

- Your venue. What does your venue say in terms of vibe?
- What colours do you like? What colours do you want to include in your wedding?
- What do you and your partner share as interests? Is there anything you would like to include in your wedding that is of interest?
- Which season are you marrying in? Do you want to tap into that feature?
- Your budget will primarily tell you what you can and can't do in terms of extravagance

- Use the internet, create a Pinterest board of all things wedding, and create a vision/mood board so you can visualise your big day
- Do the rounds, go to wedding fairs and showcase days, meet the experts in their fields, take photographs of ideas, ask for options and opinions, and don't be afraid
- Don't be pushed into something you don't want though
- Get your photos out of you and your partner. What do you see? Is there a theme there?

**Wedding themes and styles;**

**Rustic:**

Inspired by nature and the outdoors. Rustic wedding themes often include natural textures and floral and woodsy accents. Decor that evokes the countryside with its warm, cosy and laid-back details. Choosing earth tones that appear in nature, browns, oranges, reds, yellows and golds.

**Vintage:**

Remembering days of old, usually from the 1920s-1970s. This theme allows for an extraordinary and unique wedding, leaving lots of room for interpretation. Think the Victorian era meets Bridgerton. Florals, prints, chintzy and pastel shades like pinks, lilacs, lavenders, mint, lemon, soft blues and purples.

## Beach:

To pull off a beach-themed wedding, you need to incorporate all the different shades and things that being at the beach emulates. You have the sand with its beige hues and lighter tones of the natural environment. You have the ocean/sea with its turquoise, cornflower blue, and shades of sea green and blue. Then bring in your other colours, like pinks, yellows, peaches, and whites, to complement your other beach shades. Think sun, sea, sand, and seashells.

## Fairytale:

Creating a timeless celebration, bringing the romance and basing it on your favourite childhood fairytale. With elegant styling and meaningful details that have been thoughtfully planned to bring your vision to life. Create a magical, romantic atmosphere with cascading blooms, flowing fabrics and candlelight.

## Modern:

Sophisticated, refined, sleek and chic. The venue is a visual focus itself, with its decor being kept clean and simple. Think ghost chairs. Using geometric lines, monochromatic colours and evoking a less is more attitude to decor. Using on-trend colours, florals and foliage. Black for its sleek, regal feel and white to signify innocence, a perfect monochrome look for a wedding.

## Boho:

A wedding theme which is more about the styling than anything else, with its eclectic, natural, earthy feel. A bohemian theme doesn't need luxurious, glamorous decorations. It's more casual and relaxed. It brings a combination of rustic, vintage and hippie details into its design. Bohemian wedding colour palettes consist of peacock, taupe, sand, cranberry, pumpkin, violet, fuchsia, yellow, green and cyan. Think macramé, feathers and dream catchers.

**Shabby chic:**

An unconventional and unrestrictive wedding. Filled with whatever brings you joy, incorporating a soft, more opulent cottage style. Using modern things that are made to look distressed and weathered. Giving you all of your heart's desires. Florals should play a big part is this theme. Using spring and summer colours.

**Classic:**

White flowers, lots of foliage, light linens and minimal decor. These are wedding details that will never go out of style. Offering a timeless, classic wedding style.

**Garden/outdoor:**

Lots of florals, foliage and being at one with nature as much as possible, decorating the wedding in the beauty of nature. Blending bold, rustic, vintage touches to your details for an enchanting garden wedding. Summer vibes with yellow and pink, as energising shades that make people happy, are a good choice for an outdoor wedding, with its outdoor dining, flowers in your hair and dressing for the occasion, bringing the inside outside.

**Seasonal:**

Venues in winter will incorporate their Christmas decor into your ceremony and wedding reception. Winter colours of white, cream and silver. Christmas colours or red, gold and green.

Pumpkins, leaves and colours that are both warm and cool create a balance between them both for a gorgeous Autumn wedding theme. Find the mix you like for the perfect colour combination.

A summer wedding filled with bright, vibrant colours is a popular choice.

Spring into something new with warm, cool and pastel shades.

**Nautical:**

Anchors, lighthouses and boats are not the only details used for this theme. Incorporate navy blue and emerald green in your colours and stripes. Work with lots of greenery, sea accents, sea fairing foods, and decor that infuses nautical details.

**Just remember,**

Regardless of what you choose as your wedding theme, remember that beauty is in the details.

Incorporate your venue decor, and make sure it's an element of your wedding theme. Make sure everything fits nicely and blends.

Your theme should be easily recognised by your guests, it should also be personal to you both, and it should stand out.

Have fun, and don't stress. It will all come together like fitting jigsaw pieces together.

**Notes;**

# Same-sex marriages/Civil partnerships

## What is a civil partnership?

It's a legal union of 2 people who are not related to one another. Similar to a marriage, instead of saying vows, you sign a civil partnership document. Originally created for same-sex couples who were not legally allowed to marry. Now available for any couple to do.

### Here is a bit of information, rules and regulations for you:

- Same-sex couples can get married in a civil ceremony.

- Religious organisations have to agree to marry same-sex couples, and they have to be registered for same-sex marriages in order for same-sex religious ceremonies to take place. However, the Church of England and the Church of Wales do not marry same-sex couples.
- Religious organisations, or even individual ministers, do not have to legally provide a marriage service for same-sex couples.
- Same-sex couples that marry abroad, under foreign law, are recognised as being married in England and Wales.
- Countries that do not recognise same-sex marriage or civil partnerships are Russia, Turkey, Poland, and almost all Asian countries.
- Countries that do not allow same-sex marriages but do allow civil partnerships are Italy, Greece, Northern Ireland and Croatia.
- Countries that do allow same-sex marriages and civil partnerships are America, South Africa, Iceland, France,

141

Germany, Austria, Canada, Costa Rica, Colombia, Brazil, Australia, New Zealand, Portugal, Spain, Malta and all Scandinavian countries.

- Make sure you follow the rules and regulations of that country with regard to their marriage laws, make sure you have all your documentation, and check your residency rules for the country you are getting married in.
- If you have your heart set on a country that does not allow same-sex marriages or civil partnerships, you could always legally wed in the UK and then hold a symbolic blessing ceremony in your chosen country.

## Converting a same-sex civil partnership into a marriage;

Same-sex couples can convert a civil partnership document into a marriage in England and Wales. The following must apply, though:

- You've been living in the country for 28 days or over
- your civil partnership took place under the laws and regulations of England, Scotland or Wales.
- One of you is a British citizen
- You can convert your same-sex civil partnership to a marriage at a registry office, a local registration office or an approved religious setting.
- You will need to sign a "conversion to marriage" declaration at your local registry office.
- You will need your original civil partnership certificate and your ID.
- You will get a marriage certificate dated when your civil partnership was originally formed.

- You can include up to 4 parents each on your declaration, mothers, fathers, adoptive parents and step-parents.

- You cannot convert any civil partnership into a marriage in Northern Ireland, and there may be different rules in Scotland to England.

- You cannot convert an opposite-sex civil partnership to a marriage in England or Wales.

- If you formed your same-sex civil partnership here in the UK, you might be able to convert this into a marriage in some of the countries listed above if you want to do it abroad.

- If one of you has been issued a gender recognition certificate, and you were the civil partner of the person who you now wish to marry, there is no requirement for the 28-day notice period. Your notice of marriage and the marriage itself can happen on the same day.

- If a transgender person has applied for a gender recognition certificate by the gender recognition panel and it has been granted and can get a new birth certificate that reflects the gender they have now acquired. You can marry someone of the opposite sex, or same sex, in England and Wales. However, if there is no gender recognition certificate, you are legally considered to be the gender that is on your original birth certificate.

Your marriage ceremony can be held at a venue where same-sex marriages are allowed.

Don't forget to discuss the wording you want during your ceremony with the person that is conducting the ceremony.

Invite your friends and family. You do not need witnesses for your ceremony.

Go forth, and have the most spectacular wedding ceremony and enjoy every bit of it.

**Notes;**

# Alternative weddings

Outside of the norm, for the alternative people out there that like or want a fun, unique wedding. Here are your not-so-typical ideas for a wedding up your street.

## Alternative ceremonies;

## Ring warming:

Ideal for small intimate weddings but can be done with large numbers, as long as you have people in place to do some ring controlling to speed up the process of this type of addition to your ceremony, i.e. ushers/bridesmaids.

A ring-warming ceremony is where each guest is given an invitation by the person who is conducting your ceremony to hold your rings. They then say a silent prayer/blessing for you and your marriage. They then pass it on to the next guest for them to do the same. The rings are passed along at the beginning of your ceremony so that it can be completed, hopefully by the time your rings are needed for your exchanging of the rings part of your ceremony.

If you are going to worry about the rings being dropped during this and the bad luck that brings, maybe put the rings on a pillow, book, or something symbolic to you both. That way, you know they are safe.

## Unity ceremony:

This is a meaningful, symbolic ritual that is performed during your wedding, representing you both becoming a union.

Once you have exchanged vows, it is symbolic of going through a visual exchange to join you both together as one in marriage. As the spice girls say, "when 2 become 1".

Unity ceremonies like handfasting and the lighting of a unity candle are the most common rituals used, but whatever is symbolic to you both is ideal.

### Lighting a unity candle:

Before your ceremony, 3 candles are placed at the altar, 2 thinner taper candles on either side of a large church/unity candle, and one person from each family lights 1 of the taper candles. Once you have exchanged your vows, each of you uses one of the taper candles to light the unity candle at the same time. If you have children and you want them to take part in uniting as one family, get them to light a taper candle, and when it's time, they can join in with lighting the unity candle together at the same time as yourselves.

### Tying of a unity knot:

"a cord of 3 strands is not quickly broken."

Each cord represents one for you, one for your partner, and the third cord is either based on your religion, your family, your friends, your spiritual guide, or whatever is relevant to you both.

During your ceremony, you take turns braiding the cord and securing it with a knot. After your wedding, hang your cord up in your home as a reminder of the commitment and strength of you both and your marriage.

### The planting of a unity tree:

Are you symbolic of nature? Great to do if you have an outdoor wedding.

Before your ceremony, a tree is placed in a large pot near the altar; during your ceremony, you each take turns adding soil and water to the pot, nurturing the tree like you nurture your marriage. When your wedding is over, you can then take the tree home and plant it in your garden or yard.

A growing reminder of your commitment to each other.


## Sand ceremonies:

Now a modern style twist on an old ceremony tradition.

2 jars of sand representing you both; after you have exchanged your vows, you both pour your sand into an empty jar, a piece of art, a vase, or something symbolic to you both.

You could use different coloured sand for more of a statement.

Have a photograph of you both placed into a shadow box, and pour your sand into that. This can then be hung in your home as a reminder of your union.

And if you have children, you could each have your own sand jar to pour into your empty item all at the same time to unify your family.

For extra memories, why not jar up sand that is relevant to you, like take a sample from the beach where you live, or come from, from an area where you like to go walking or on holiday? It is a meaningful and sentimental touch to your wedding. You could even exchange your vows whilst pouring your sand for the extra sentiment. Make your ceremony something more.


## Sealing of an anniversary gift box:

A dual celebration, serving as a meaningful joining on your wedding day and also an anniversary gift in years to come.

Have a box made, maybe with your names and your wedding date on it. Before your wedding, and in privacy, write your partner a love letter, maybe share some memories in the form of photographs too, seal these up and place them in your box.

Maybe put a bottle of wine/champagne in there for you both to share on your anniversary. Decide on what anniversary you are going to wait to open your box on, i.e. five or ten years. Maybe get wine/champagne that ages well.

During your ceremony, your items will be in the box, and you can both seal it shut together. Signifying the meaning behind your wine/champagne choice, unifying your love for one another. And on your anniversary, you can reminisce on your wedding day, enjoying your glass of something nice.

**Alternative wedding flowers:**

Fun options for anyone wanting to forgo the traditional wedding bouquet altogether;

- Carry a lit candle lantern
- Carry a balloon bouquet, maybe in heart shapes, or balloons in a colour theme, to your wedding
- Have a feather bouquet or pampas grass bouquet instead
- Wear a fur muff, and don't carry anything at all
- Hold a mason jar with some loose flowers in it
- Have a button bouquet, a brooch bouquet, or a paper flower bouquet, instead
- Carry a hoop of flowers, foliage, pampas, or a wreath
- Wear a statement necklace or dramatic headpiece for some show-stopping attraction

**Make a guest bouquet.**

Get your guests to bring a single-stem flower of their choice.

As you enter your wedding ceremony, greet your guests, acknowledge their floral gift, and as each guest gives you their flower assemble your flowers as you go; by the time you get to the altar, you will have a bouquet of loose flowers, that will have some form of meaning, and you would have acknowledged all your guests and spent a few seconds with them on the way to the altar. They will love this. You could then utilise your flowers at the reception in a vase and take them home with you after your wedding and appreciate them for days after in your home.

**Alternative wedding themes:**

Always dreamt of having your wedding to suit yourselves? Something mind-blowing, creative and unusual? Break the norm on wedding traditions and do things your own way, for you both!

Here are some unique ideas for alternative wedding themes;

- Fantasy movie theme, you have Lord of the rings, Pirates of the Caribbean, Dr Who, Hunger Games, Harry Potter, Star Wars, Star Trek, and Game of Thrones.

- Dawn of the dead theme, for all the zombie apocalypse thrillers out there.

- Festival, music, bands, carnival, rainbow-type theme

- Superhero themes, you have Superman, Spider-Man, Batman, The Avengers, Fantastic four, Marvel theme, Pixar theme, you can literally go on and on.

- Disney themes, Alice in Wonderland, Beauty and the beast, Little mermaid, Frozen, Snow White, Cinderella, Mary Poppins, Pocahontas.

- Dark, Gothic, enchanting themes, fairies, witches, Halloween, all the dark forest, think Maleficent, into the woods vibes.

- Steampunk theme. Vikings. Medieval, retro-inspired theme.

- Robin Hood, Wizard of Oz, The Great Gatsby, and Country Western are all great movie themes.

- Sport-themed. Dance themed.

- Celestial theme, with the sun, moon and stars guiding you.

- Historical theme, downtown abbey meets bridgerton.

- Costume party theme, get all your guests involved.

- Whether you take snippets from your ideal wedding theme, and have it mingling in and around your wedding day, with touches here and there, maybe in a themed cake, themed invitations, or themed shoes.
- Or you go the full hog, and your theme is your wedding, and you embrace it to its fullest. It's your day, your way.

**Alternative touches:**

Here are some other alternatives for you to break tradition with.

- Instead of a first dance, have a first song or a first karaoke session.
- Write a note on your shoe for your partner and guests to see.
- Wear a trouser suit instead of a dress.
- Have more than one person give you away.
- Have a self-serve buffet instead of a formal sit-down meal.
- Have different desserts in the middle of your tables as centrepieces. Guests can tuck in after their meal.
- Have a dance-off instead of the first dance.
- Take your guests and go bowling, have a round of golf, go clay pigeon shooting, do archery, or axe throwing, to name a few things to do besides your traditional wedding arrangements.
- Go to a theme park as part of your celebrations.
- Have a wine-tasting evening.
- Have a family member or friend be the celebrant for your wedding.
- Do opposite colours to your bridesmaids. Get them in white or ivory, and you do any other colour.

Whatever you decide on, it can be the only part of your wedding that you adapt from the traditional, or it can be all of your weddings. You can blend it all together and stand out from the crowds, or just have pockets of change here and there.

Your day, your way! You decide.

**Notes;**

# Cultural differences

Wedding traditions from any country or culture have all got these things in common, all of the traditions are rooted in history, and primarily the meaning behind them all is to wish the newlyweds good fortune, fidelity and fertility. So no matter how unique, sweet or totally off the scale the traditions are, the meaning behind them is pure.

Here are some of the traditions that certain countries and cultures from around the world believe in. Some you may have to adopt certain traditions if you are getting married in that country. Also, your partner may be from that country, or their culture believes in certain things, and you can pay tribute to that at your wedding. Embrace the culture.


**Greece;**

To ensure a sweet life and a prosperous financial future for her marriage, the bride should hide a sugar cube in her glove and a gold coin in her shoe.

If the groom holds a piece of iron in his pocket, it will help ward off evil spirits.

A Greek wedding will have good luck if there is an odd number of guests attending. This stems from the number 3 representing the Holy Trinity, the Father, the Son and the Holy Ghost. Continuing with the rule of 3, the wedding rings are exchanged and blessed 3 times. Wine is sipped from the common cup 3 times. All of these actions represent a successful union and marriage.

The Stefana (marital crown) is worn by the bride and groom and consists of flowers, foliage and precious metals and is joined together by a ribbon. It symbolises the union of the bride and groom, and as they walk around the altar 3 times which represents your journey through life together, the priest will bless them both.

The light of Christ is held in the form of a candle throughout the ceremony.

There are also dates, months and times of the year that are said to bring good luck if you marry then. January and June are considered to be the better months for marriage.

Don't forget all the Greek dancing, the holding of hands and the dancing in circles.

Panemorfi


## Scandinavian countries;

Swedish brides are given a gold coin from their father and a silver coin from their mother. These go in the bride's shoes, and they represent a life of good luck, good fortune and prosperity.

There is also a Swedish custom for the guests to kiss the newlyweds.

It's tradition for the bride and groom to walk down the aisle together and for the bride to keep her bridal bouquet.

Norwegian brides must wear silver and gold in their wedding crown, with small gem charms in it also, so when she walks, it makes a tinkling sound which wards off evil spirits.

A traditional native bunad suit is worn by the groom and the groomsmen. Other wedding guests can wear their traditional bunad suits too. The bride will wear a dress variation of the bunad.

Rye and barley grains are thrown at the newlyweds to celebrate their union. The newlyweds try to catch as much as they can. The more they collect, the brighter their future will be.

There are lots of traditional cakes that are involved in a Norwegian wedding.

In all Scandinavian countries, speeches and toasts are a big thing, where family members and friends can all tell stories of the couple and bring joy and laughter to the day. They are spread out across the wedding reception rather than just being at one particular time.

Danish brides will wear the traditional white dress and veil, but they also must wear something red. Red is symbolic to love, and in Denmark, it also wards off evil spirits.

Danish grooms always choose and buy the bride's bouquet.

A Gate of Honour is placed around the door to the bride's house on her wedding day. This is made up of pine branches and flowers. It is made by friends and family of the bride. It is also re-created on their 25th wedding anniversary.

Danish newlyweds must dance before midnight. The bride's dance is called the brudevals, which is like a waltz, and then the groom's dance is followed by the male guests, where they will take their socks off.

The traditional wedding cake must be eaten by all the guests. Everybody must get a slice otherwise, this will resort in the newlyweds having a bad marriage.

Viking Norse traditions, weddings only take place on a Friday, Frigg's day/Freya's day. This is from the Norse goddess beliefs of fertility and love, and if you married on any other day, it would be a bad omen.

Pre-wedding preparations for both the bride and the groom were held in the run-up to their wedding. This involved preparing the couple for married life; brides would get rid of their old clothing and the jewellery that objectified them as virgins and bathed. And the grooms had to prove their manly hood by grave robbing a family sword.

Rings and swords are exchanged in the wedding ceremony.

They also had a feast fit for kings on their wedding day.

Skon

## Ireland;

For brides with Irish ancestry or for Irish brides, their dresses are embellished with Celtic symbols like knots, crosses or shamrocks. Irish lace can also be added to the dress, headpiece or veil. The grooms wear an Irish kilt representing their country and district. And wear a full formal kilt outfit.

Ireland's traditional colour was originally blue, so don't be surprised if blue elements surface at the wedding. It symbolises luck, fidelity and commitment to your partner.

Irish luck is seen in shamrocks and horseshoes, the right side up.

Irish linen handkerchiefs embroidered with a shamrock carried on your wedding day are also seen as a sign of good luck. And should be sewn into a bonnet as part of your first child's christening outfit.

Irish pipers, Celtic harpists, handfasting, Irish dancers, Claddagh rings, ringing of the bells, and Bells of Ireland flowers in the bride's bouquet. All feature in traditional Irish weddings, bringing luck, prosperity and culture to the wedding day.

Alainn

## Scotland;

The groom and groomsmen will traditionally wear a Scottish tartan kilt in the clan of the family name, and the bride would also incorporate this tartan into a shawl and sash to wear with her dress or have ribbons in her bouquet to match.

Scottish brides and grooms literally tie the knot on their wedding day. Each person provides a strip of their clan tartan, the fabric is tied around their wrists during the wedding ceremony, and as the pair pull their hands apart, the fabric tightens and eventually, with some movements to get their hands free, the fabric forms into a knot. Representing the coming together of the 2 clans. And it is a great momentum for their wedding day and something to treasure.

Scottish luck in weddings is also paved with Scottish bagpipers.

A dram of whisky is drunk by the bride and groom to seal the marriage. This is drinking from what is called a Quaich. It is to be held with 2 hands, and as it is traditionally showing the 2 clans joining as 1, it shows trust, honour and respect. The bride drinks first, and the groom drinks next. Then it would be passed round the rest of the clan leaders.

Bonnie


## Wales;

Myrtle, the herb that symbolises love, is always included in a Welsh bride's bouquet; the bride will give a cutting of myrtle to her bridesmaids for them to plant it in their gardens, the first one to have it bloom will be the next one to get married.

It is believed that if a Welsh bride is woken up on her wedding day by birdsong, it is especially lucky. Folklore believes that God sent birds to represent angels, spirit guides or animal totems, as birds celebrate the dawns chorus with cheerful song, giving praise to the heavens above, so hearing birdsongs on the morning of your wedding would be the universe praising your decision in your new chapter.

When a Welshman fell in love and wanted to propose, he would carve a love spoon from wood and present it to his beloved, and it would feature a key to represent that she had the key to his heart, and it would have beads attached which would symbolise the number of children he hoped to have.

Hardd

## France;

French weddings are a celebration of the union of two families, both equal in terms of customs, an equal amount of guests attending, and an equal number of witnesses, a true symbol of unity.

To be legally married in France, the marriage ceremony must be performed by the mayor in the town hall as a public event, with the doors open for anyone to oppose the marriage. Spiritual and religious weddings can be done afterwards. This is called a La Mairie; it is part tradition and part legal.

To enter the ceremony, the groom will walk down the aisle with his mother, the flower girls will drop petals, and then the bride will walk down with her father. Laurel leaves will be scattered outside the church to symbolise their achievement. The cake is a traditional French croquembouche, and the wedding itself will take place over a day and a half with all its festivities.

Belle

## Spain;

Spanish couples that are due to wed have chosen godparents that they have known their entire lives. They are their bridal party, that's it.

Wedding rings for Spanish women are worn on the right hand, and the engagement ring is worn on the left hand, and normally they are made of gold.

In Spanish catholic weddings, the couple is given 13 coins, known as the arras or the unity coins, they represent Jesus and his 12 apostles, and it's meant to bring the couple good fortune in their marriage ahead.

Wedding cakes are cut with swords, dried rice and rose petals are thrown at the bride and groom to wish them prosperity and fertility as newlyweds, and there is lots of dancing and sangria.

Bello

## Italy;

The luckiest day for Italians to get married is a Sunday, and the unluckiest day is a Friday.

To bring luck to their marriage and to ward off evil spirits, the groom will carry a small piece of iron in his suit pocket, and the bride will make a small rip in her veil and is not allowed to see herself in the mirror on the morning of her wedding.

The groom pays for the bridal bouquet.

After the nuptials, the newlyweds break a glass vase, and the number of shards it breaks into represents how many happy years the newlyweds have in their marriage.

Newlyweds are showered with rice to symbolise fertility after their nuptials, and all the guests are given a chance to congratulate the newlyweds on their marriage.

The groom removes the bride's garter during the wedding reception and throws it to the wedding guests. If the bride isn't wearing a garter, he throws her right shoe instead.

It is traditional in Italy that male guests give the bride money in exchange for a dance. And during the couple's first dance, the couple hold streamers in their hands, the guests hold the other ends of the streamers, and as they move around the dance floor, the couple is wrapped up in streamers to signify well wishes. The guests also perform the traditional La Tarantella dance with the bride and groom in the centre. Lots of Italian wine will be drunk.

Bellissima


## Asian countries;

Muslim weddings:

Muslim women have intricate henna designs done on their hands and feet for the ceremony, it must complement their whole attire, and the bride must have the most intricate hand mehndi design, above all the other women in attendance.

The baat-pakki rasm is the Muslim version of an engagement; although rare, the couple may exchange engagement rings at this time and then later replace them with their wedding rings. Once engaged, the two families start organising the dholki events, which there are several of them. After the dholki events, the Nikkah ceremony in the mosque takes place, with close family and friends to pray for the well-being of the couple due to marry. After this event, the couple's parents organise separate events for the couple where it's customary to apply a blend of Mehndi to them to wish them well in their celebrations.

The wedding is known as the Baraat or the Shaadi, which is the actual event of the wedding. And the completion of the wedding ceremony is called the Rukhsati.

Muslim weddings are the grandest and most community-celebrated events, and they value wedding traditions so much.

## Buddhist weddings;

The matchmaking process is the first step. The boys' families make the proposal; horoscopes have to be matched, and then the wedding preparations can begin once the families are in agreement. The families agree on a date, in which they consult the Kıkas; they also decide on a date for the bride to leave the paternal home, and the colour of the dresses to be worn on the wedding day is also decided.

The engagement ceremony is held, which is called the Nangchangor Chessian. Once the celebration of this is done, and the Kikas is consulted again to set a final wedding date, the couple usually lives in the bride's house till the wedding.

Wedding attire must comply with the culture. The bride wears a dress called a Bhaku, with jewellery. The groom also wears a Bhaku, but it isn't as long as the bride's.

Buddhist weddings are small affairs. The ritual religious part is completed at the temple on the morning of the wedding. Then the groom's family provide the trays of food, drink, and cakes. The trays brought will be either 6 or 9 trays only. One tray will be candles for the bride and groom to light up together to symbolise their union. They do this at the shrine of Lord Buddha, which is also decorated with flowers and incense sticks. Hymns will be recited once here at the shrine. The bride and groom recite their vows, and a red paste is applied on their foreheads by the monk, symbolising their union.

There is lots of dancing and music at the wedding to celebrate.

The couple leaves the bride's paternal home on the date stated in their Kikas.

## Hindu weddings;

Begin with the lagna patrika, which is the formal engagement ceremony and announcement of the intended marriage. The couple exchange vows and decides on a date.

15 days before the wedding, certain rituals are undertaken, and a thread is tied to the groom and his parent's hands, asking the gods for safe passage on the wedding day. A pre-wedding ceremony called the Pithi is undertaken in which a turmeric paste is applied to the couple to ward off evil spirits and to wish them blessings and good luck. The bride has a Mehndi party in which henna is applied to her hands and feet, and the other women are in attendance at her wedding. It is supposed to bring luck and good health.

The sangeet festivities begin, which is a pre-wedding event of song and dance enjoyed by friends and family. Bringing in the two families and their union.

On the day of the wedding, the baraat, which is the groom's arrival at the wedding ceremony, involves lots of dancing and singing for the groom's procession. The pokwanu takes place next, which is the bride's family welcoming the groom to theirs, and a mark is made on the groom's forehead. The bride's entrance is next underneath a canopy generally joined by the bride's brothers, aunts, and uncles.

The wedding takes place under a mandap and is known to mean the foundation and forming of marriage. No shoes are to be worn under the mandap.

The couple is tied together by their hands with the groom's scarf to symbolise them joining together, and this is also part of the wedding ceremony.

To honour their wedding ceremony to the god of fire, the couple will offer handfuls of rice to honour Agni. This is called the havan.

The couple will exchange floral garlands made up of jasmine, marigolds and bright-coloured roses.

The seven steps around the circle of sacred fire will take place whilst the couple exchange their vows and prayers, each vow representing a stage in their marriage that they will encounter. The seven steps represent food, strength, prosperity, family, offspring, health and friendship. Once the seven steps are complete, the couple is considered married.

The mangal sutra sacred necklace is placed on the bride and shows people she is married. This can only be removed if she becomes widowed. Once the necklace is adorned, the groom will apply a vermilion red cosmetic powder to her head. This is known as a sindoor.

The families give blessings to the couple. As the couple bid their farewell.

Piao liang


**Eastern European countries:**

Romanian weddings;

Usually, take place in their village, the food is usually prepared at home by the bride and groom's extended family, and the weddings usually have hundreds of guests.

The homemade wine and plum brandy are up for grabs, and there is usually no dress code per se, and they will have local traditional music and lots of dancing.

The couple officially gets married at the starea civila either the morning of the wedding or a few days before their church ceremony. They have to attend that in order to be legally married. The church ceremony can take up to two hours, and you have to stand for the full duration. Sometimes the wedding can go over two days due to the ceremonies.

The kidnapping of the bride is a big event at a Romanian wedding. The bride is kidnapped, usually by close friends, and the groom is then asked for a ransom to bring the bride back. This originally involved money, but now fun things like singing karaoke or doing a funny dance are part of the ransom. It's a big tradition in Romania.

### Bulgarian weddings;

If the father agrees to the marriage, the groom must ask the bride three times for her hand in marriage. If she answers yes three times, this is considered to be an engagement. At the engagement feast, the details of the wedding are arranged. This is considered to be legally binding from here on in.

Most weddings in Bulgaria are on a Sunday, the Thursday before the wedding, the bride's mother must make the ritual pitka bread for the wedding, and the groom's best man must make the wedding banner. On the morning of the wedding, the groom's family and friends gather at his house, the procession of family then goes to the best man's house to collect him, then the procession goes on to the bride's house, there's wine, food, candles, the bride's veil, once at the bride's house the merrymaking carries on, the bridesmaid attempts to put the veil on the brides head, the bride must refuse twice and accept it on the third time. The bride and groom are led outside, and the procession starts at the church. On their right foot first, the ceremony begins.

The groom's mother lays a white hand-woven cloth at the door of the reception for the newlyweds to enter, and she throws flowers on their path. This symbolises health and happiness in their life together. The groom's mother then feeds the newlyweds a sweet honey cake and wine to wish them a sweet life together. She then holds a loaf of pitka bread over her head and invites the couple to pull at either end of it. Whoever pulls the bigger part of the bread will have the bigger role to play in their family.

## Polish weddings;

Blessings for the soon-to-be newlyweds begin on the Saturday before the wedding. At the bride's home, family members give the couple their special blessings, with holy water, crucifixes, and spoken blessings.

Once the church ceremony is concluded the couple make their way to the reception where their parents welcome them with bread and salt, which represent the hopes that the couple will never feel hunger and that they will overcome life's struggles when confronted with difficulties. The couple is then served one shot of water and one shot of vodka. They don't know which is which; they have to knock them back, and whoever gets the vodka is meant to be the dominant partner in the relationship. The glasses are thrown on the floor, and if they smash, it is considered to be good luck.

The removal of the bride's veil is a polish tradition of a bride's first night as a married woman. The veil is thrown, and whoever catches it is said to be the next bride. A polish bride's hair is woven into braids with flowers, myrtle and rosemary. It symbolises her maidenhood.

Polish weddings can last over a full weekend, with all their festivities, music and dancing.

Piekny

## American weddings;

The bridal bouquet toss is a long-standing American tradition. Whoever catches the bouquet is said to marry next.

American bridesmaids' dresses all have to be the same colour to confuse the evil spirits.

For their something old, Americans will choose a wedding poem of sorts to be read out at their wedding.

Jumping the broom tradition is still a popular tradition in America. It symbolises sweeping away evil spirits, past loves, and the old you whilst also representing jumping into your new life together and setting up your house.

Beautiful

Embrace the culture of your native country, give it justice, do your ancestors proud, go the whole hog, or take bits out and just utilise those, give the old traditions a new twist if you must, or endure the ways of old. Whatever you decide to do, whether it's for you both, or your partner, enjoy it. I haven't researched every country in the world, and I send my apologies if your heritage isn't on this list, feel free to get in touch and I will research and respond to your questions, queries and details.

If you're attending a wedding with cultural differences, observe what other guests are doing, and follow the flow of the ceremony. The officiant of the wedding will explain the order of events and each step's significance in multi-cultural weddings. As a guest, you are probably not expected to participate in certain rituals. Once the ceremony is over, remain in your seat as typically, the family members will file out immediately after the couple.

**Notes;**

# Finer details

Your plans are coming together, you've put deposits down on some of your suppliers, you are making arrangements that resemble your personalities, and you are putting your own stamp on things. Trust your instincts, you will both remember your perfect moments, and you will have memories to last a lifetime.

But just in case you have missed some of the finer details, here are some of the things you may want to consider and add to your to-do list if you want;

## Confetti;

Do you want guests to throw confetti as you leave your ceremony? Are you going to provide it, or are you relying on guests to remember to bring some? You could put a pouch of confetti on every other chair at your ceremony or have a basket of loose confetti for people to grab on their way out of the ceremony.

## Unplugged;

Do you want guests to be able to take photographs on their phones? Maybe put things on social media from your wedding on a dedicated wedding app? This can be shared by everyone then.

On the flip side, phones can be a distraction, and you could ask guests to go unplugged, get them to put their phones away and enjoy the day instead. This also means your photographer can do their job. You could get a sign stating either of your choices, so guests are aware.

**Insurance;**

If you're marrying abroad, you may want to take out wedding insurance as well as comprehensive travel insurance, as a standard policy won't cover everything for the potential problems that may arise whilst abroad.

In fact, you may want to take out wedding insurance anyway. It will cover standard things like venue cancellation, damage to an outfit, loss of rings, food poisoning etc. check the small print to see what is definitely included in your policy.

Your wedding insurance won't cover you for your honeymoon, and you will have to take out separate travel insurance for that.

**Travelling abroad;**

Are you taking a wedding dress abroad? Speak to your airline, tour operator or travel agent. You may be able to take it as hand luggage. Some airlines actually let you hang the dress up in a dress bag.

Maybe discuss where you bought the dress from as to how you should pack it and fold it. If it's going in luggage, you want to limit the creases.

Maybe consider a lightweight dress, beach-friendly, one that can go in your hold luggage.

And for the groom, consider a lightweight suit instead of a morning suit. This also may be hung up in a dress bag too.

**Table seating;**

Probably one of the biggest hurdles you will have to overcome if you have a formal seating arrangement for your wedding breakfast. Here are a few suggestions to get guests talking and ways in which to break the ice for your guests too.

- Mix up the tables, and get creative with your sitting plan; who said Aunt Tilly had to be next to Aunt Floss?
- Find things that some guests have in common, travel connections, past connections, and maybe parts of each family have similar backgrounds. Food is always a great topic and gets people talking.
- Photographs of both families around the venue are always an icebreaker, especially if there are comedy photographs.

## Schedule;

Timing is everything, you don't want to miss out on anything on your wedding day, so it would be a shame if you run out of time to do a certain part of your day. Maybe have a timing schedule to stick to? Make sure everything and everyone runs smoothly.

If there's one thing that is going to run over, it's the speeches. You may want to get the people who are making speeches to time themselves when they are practising. Maybe consider a time limit on toasts? Just a suggestion, if you have speeches before your meal, you don't want your guests to go hungry.

## Exits;

If you're jetting off to your honeymoon straight after your celebrations, you might want to consider an exit strategy so you can be where you need to be at the right time. You don't want to miss your travel connections.

Unless backdoor boogies are an option, you might want to say your goodbyes to your loved ones.

**Tasters and trials;**

Food tasting, wine tasting, cake tasting, and dessert tasting may not always be possible, and it certainly will depend on the type of caterers you're having, keep in regular contact with them to ensure there are no surprises on your day.

Hair and make-up trials may also not be possible. You may have to pay for these in addition to your original price as well, you may want to practice on yourself to see what you think, give yourself some ideas, keep pictures of your favourites, and if you're marrying abroad you may want to take pictures of your styles so they can see, you may also need a translator if they don't speak your language.

**Essentials;**

You may want to provide certain essentials for your guests in the toilets, things that may have been forgotten, or maybe left in their hotel room. Here are a few suggestions,

- Plasters, deodorants, perfume, sanitary products, hair brushes, dry shampoo, hairspray, hair grips, pocket tissues, mini sewing kit, dental hygiene products, sexual health products, make-up products, sun tan lotion.
- This also applies if you want to provide comfier footwear for people to dance in, like flip flops or some other flat shoe. Make sure you provide in various sizes too.
- If you are getting married outdoors, you may want to provide a few blankets in case it gets very cold at night.
- If you're hanging up your dress and your bridesmaid's dresses, you may want to hang them on bridal hangers. Maybe with their names on so you know whose dress is whose.

171

- Whilst your getting ready you may want to be in bridal dressing gowns, again you could get them named.

**Thank you's;**

After all your celebrations are over, and you're back home, make sure you send out thank you cards to your guests, don't fail at the last hurdle. You should send these out within three months after the wedding.

**Don't forget;**

To match your colour scheme with all your minor details, like your stationery, napkins, and table runners, match your decor, so it's all set up nicely.

Signs, if you do not want guests to be on social media, tell them if you are marrying outdoors. Guests may need to know where the toilets are, the bar, and the dance floor.

Let guests know where they can park at the venue, and also provide directions to the venue if the transport is not provided.

Ask your venue if there is any outdoor heating, especially if it's cold at night or you are getting married in the winter, things like fire pits or patio heaters.

Likewise, if it's too hot, is their air conditioning provided or fans?

Are you changing into another outfit? Or maybe changing into something less restricted, maybe you want to be in comfier shoes in the evening, don't forget to take them then, your shoes you could hide under your top table, so they are ready for you to change into.

Jetting off to your honeymoon straight after your wedding? Don't forget to pack for it before your wedding so you are all prepared and ready to go straight away.


**Notes;**

# Suppliers

Whether you hire suppliers to help you with one particular wedding arrangement or whether you need certain suppliers there throughout your wedding day, here is a list of certain suppliers you may need for your wedding.

It will also give you a brief outline of what they can provide for your wedding and some hints and tips on how to choose your suppliers.

## Photographer;

A photographer will have different packages for you to choose from. Depending on what you are looking for, they will be able to offer part-day packages, where you will be able to choose a time for the photographer to start taking photographs and finish. Some photographers will go by the hours required. And then you have the full-day package.

Ask yourself, what do you want the photographer to photograph? Are you both getting ready in the morning, getting out of the car, the ceremony, the cake cutting, the first dance, your meal?

Then ask yourself, what kind of photographs are you looking to have, natural, unposed, non-traditional, unique, formal, or traditional?

Things to ask your photographer;

Do they provide your photographs digitally too?

Do they provide a pre-wedding shoot?

How many photographs do you get?

How many photographers will there be on the day?

Are you required to pay for their meal if staying for the day?

Are you provided with a photograph album?

What extra services do they provide? E.g. photo booth, drone, Ariel shots

Choose your photographer carefully. They should have a good reputation. Ask for samples of their work, and try and meet them face to face. You should have a rapport with them, they are going to be photographing you on one of the most important days of your life, and you want the memories in years to come.

Make sure you give your photographer's details to your church if you are getting married in a church and the venue. Some of your other suppliers may swap details with the photographer so they can share social media advertisements and tag each other in your photographs.

To find a wedding photographer near you, try www.findaweddingphotographer.co.uk

You also may want to ask your photographer if they belong to the guild of photographers.

**Videographer;**

Having your wedding filmed means you can watch your big day back and relive it in years to come. You will be able to see the things you might not have registered on your actual day with it being so busy. You may have missed some of your guest's reactions to you walking down the aisle, or you missed Aunt Flo tearing up at the speeches. It's to reminisce on the things you did not have the time to take in on the day itself.

A videographer should provide you with a highlighted summary of the day itself over a period of rolling time. It should be fully edited and should include the main events like the ceremony, speeches, first dance etc. They should also provide this on a hard drive or USB so you can access it from several devices.

Videographers will have different packages similar to a photographer. They will go on whether you want them there for the full day, part day, or only doing certain parts of your wedding. Usually, a four, six or eight-hour package.

Discuss with your videographer what you want to capture, and make sure they know that if you want to achieve something, in particular, they have to have the bravery to get the camera angled in a way to get the job done, and it may involve them getting into risky situations. Do they have the creative ability and the attention to detail to pull off the imaginable in order to get the right shot?

A videographer must be organised, have great time management, they must be able to work under pressure, and be able to work in all weathers. You want them to be able to capture the beauty of your day through their lens.

When asked, If there's one thing a wedding couple regrets after their wedding, it is not having their day filmed, so they can relive their day and watch it in years to come.

**Prop hire;**

Some suppliers may moonlight into other areas with the kind of products they provide, so it's always good to ask exactly what they can offer, but for most event hire agencies, prop hire companies will be your go-to people for those extra details you want to have for your wedding.

If you do hire any electrical equipment, make sure they have been pat tested and that all of the suppliers are up to date with their public liability insurance.

Advise your venue of any additional products you will be bringing into their residence and that you get their agreement on this too.

Here is an outline of the kind of products you will be able to hire out;

- Giant garden games, traditional and circus-like games, and indoor games like casino roulette tables.

- Unique lighting decor, for instance, starlit ceilings, festoon lighting, led curtains, chandeliers, and hanging light installation.

- Light-up letters and neon signs led dance floors.

- Mobile bars come in a variety of setups, VW camper vans, rustic wooden bars, and caravans. They usually bring the bar, the staff, the drinks, and the glassware. Check with your hiring company if they do.

- Firework displays.

- Crockery, glassware companies, in vintage style or modern.

- Balloons in the form of balloon hoops, backdrops, and table staggers.

- Furniture hire companies, will hire out things like tables, chairs, lounging areas, fire pits, picnic benches and other furniture requirements.

- Wedding stylists, these companies will feature chair covers, sashes, centrepieces, doughnut walls, table runners, table cloths, napkins, flower walls, other styles of backdrops, post boxes, candy carts, and sweet tables.

- Vintage decor companies featuring rustic signs, vintage crockery, vintage trunks/suitcases, and deck chairs.

- Marquee companies and other outdoor event hire companies for things like tipis, yurts, tents, don't forget your portable toilets too, and generators for venues like barns, marquees and yurts, if required, for things that require electricity.

**Hairdressers;**

Whether you are going to your own salon itself to have your hair done or getting a mobile hairdresser to come to your venue on your wedding day, or even maybe doing your hair yourself. Get some pictures together of styles you like, and ask yourself what theme you are having. If, say, rustic, would a free-flowing hairstyle suit that theme rather than a formal look? Get some ideas together to show your stylist.

For those who are not doing it themselves. There are a few questions for you to think about.

Decide who is having their hair done for the day. Is it just you? Are bridesmaids included? Mums?

Are you paying for it all if you're including your bridal party?

Are you best having a hair trial?

Are you wearing a veil? Is it a forward-facing veil that goes over your face? Or is it a bit of both? Front and back veil.

Are you wearing any other jewellery in your hair? Tiara? Headband? Clip?

Are you having flowers put into your hair? Or wearing a floral crown?

Play around yourself and see what you like. Get your bridesmaids around and have a hair trial night.

Don't leave it till your wedding day to try something new. That will lead to a lot of unnecessary stress, and if you have your hair coloured, please don't do this the night before either, just in case of any head stains. You would hate yourself for it if something like that was to happen, so don't put yourself in any unnecessary circumstances.

## Make-up artist;

If you are doing this yourself, you will know what products you like, I wouldn't try anything new on the day just in case of any reactions or irritations, and I wouldn't try a new technique or a new look on your wedding day either, you will put yourself under a lot of pressure. If you are going to try a new look, practice in the coming weeks before your wedding, try a new look, see what you might like for your special day, take pictures of ideal looks, give yourself time, and practice some more so on your wedding day, it will just flow.

If you are hiring a make-up artist, make sure they can come to your venue on your wedding day, you don't want to be travelling really on your day. Always go with some pictures in mind of what you like, especially if you haven't managed to go for a make-up trial first. Again don't go for something that is totally different to what you would normally do without trialling it first. Make sure you are offered a skin allergy test the week before your wedding just to make sure you are not going to have an allergic reaction to some of the products the artist may use on you.

Make sure there is plenty of time if you are not the only person having your make-up done.

Are you and your bridal party having their make-up done?

Will they use a setting spray, so you don't necessarily have to touch anything up apart from your lipstick?

Are you paying for everyone's makeup to be done?

Are you all going for the same look?

Maybe you could go for your hair and make-up trial on the same day, so you can see it all together, utilise this moment and maybe have a friends night out whilst you're all glammed up, or a date night with your partner.

179

## Stationery;

Here is a brief overview of what stationery you might need on the run-up to your wedding and on your wedding day itself, whether you are making these yourself or hiring someone to do it all for you;

Save the dates, invitations, rsvp, directions, gift list, order of service, welcome signs, table plan, table names or numbers, place cards, menus, thank you cards, postbox, and memory signs.

You may want to follow the same colour theme and design with your stationery throughout so it all matches.

Suppose you send your rsvp, directions, and gift list with your invitations. Don't forget to label when you want your rsvp back, and you may also want to ask in your invites somewhere if anyone has any dietary requirements that you need to know about. Maybe get them to write it on their rsvp.

Your order of service, you could get away with it being every other chair.

Regarding your place cards, may I suggest you put what the person has ordered off the menu on the back of the place card so it is easier for the waitress/waiter to see what they are having and also any food allergies.

## Florist;

A wedding florist will provide you with all your floristry requirements. These will include;

Bridal bouquets, bridesmaids bouquets, flower girl arrangements, male buttonholes, ladies corsages, thank you bouquets, table displays, cake flowers, room decorations, flowers on arches.

Your florist will attend your venue to put in place any decor that needs to be arranged for you. They should provide you with pins for your buttonholes too.

Some florists will only work with fresh flowers, so it is best to check if you want artificial flowers, dried flowers or anything else.

If you're getting married abroad and taking artificial flowers with you, make sure they are packed correctly to ease any damage.

If you are getting married around any peak season, such as Valentine's Day, Mother's Day, or Christmas, be warned your flower prices will be a lot higher at those times.

If you have a look at the British flower association and the good florist guide, they will give you an insight into florists within your area.

**Babysitters;**

If you want more of an adults-only evening reception, or even just to be able to enjoy yourselves without having to worry about your children's whereabouts and what they are up to, maybe even you don't want to lumber family members or friends with the task of childminding. You want everyone to have a good time, but young children, and babies, need attention and sleep.

Hire in a babysitting service, someone who can take the children to the quiet living quarter or hotel suite, read them stories, bathe them, feed them and get them off to bed, and they would have to stick around until you return from your evening function.

And if you have guests that have children but you don't, let's say, maybe give them the suggestion of a babysitter so they can enjoy themselves too.

Please check that the childcare service provider you use is qualified and Ofsted registered.

To find out about local babysitters or childcare services in the area of your wedding, check out www.childcare.co.uk

## Pet sitters;

If you are marrying at a venue that houses animals that you can pet, or you are using a service that provides an animal-type attraction or service on your wedding day, then these providers will have everything in place for those animals already.

However, if you want your dog to be your ring bearer, or your venue allows dogs in the hotel rooms, and you do not want to leave them at home.

Then a pet-sitting service may be what you need to hire. They will be able to walk your dogs, take them out to do their business, feed them, water them, and generally look after them during your day.

They will more than likely charge by the hour. Please make sure they have all the credentials needed to do the job.

To find out about pet-sitting services in the area and what they can provide for you on your wedding day, please check out the following;

www.trustedhousesitters.com

www.care.com

www.pawshake.co.uk

Any supplier you use, for whatever requirements you need, make sure they have the credentials, insurance and everything in place to provide that service.

Make sure they have your details in case they need to get in touch with you and make sure your venue has the details of all the suppliers that will be doing things for your wedding.

Make sure your supplier knows the times from when they can arrange things at your venue if required.

Do your homework, and read the reviews. Word of mouth is the greatest form of feedback.

**Notes;**

# Animals and your wedding

This will really depend on your venue choice and what theme you are actually doing for your wedding. If you are getting married at a farm that houses animals, amazing. If you are getting married in the city in a 5 star hotel, maybe not.

Always best to check with your venue what you can and cannot do; it is quite a new thing to have animals included at a wedding, so not all venues will be up to date yet, and for some, it won't be part of their ideals.

If you are getting married at the likes of a farm, barn, or in the countryside somewhere, and they have a small holding of animals, the likelihood is they will have staff on hand to help with pictures and the mingling of animals and your guests.

If you're getting ready at home with your pets, you've got all the snuggly pet pictures you care to take. You may want to do this before you get in your dress, though.

Don't fancy travelling to your venue in a car? Then why not a horse-drawn carriage? If you have a love of horses and travelling like a royal, this could be your answer.

Some venues, registrars and celebrants will allow dog ring bearers or even just to have your pooch attend your wedding. Important to consider if your dog has the right temperament for all the guests and attention and if your animal can cope with all the emotions of the day. You may want to consider a pet service to keep your pooch entertained whilst you enjoy your wedding.

Don't want to put your pooch through that on your wedding day? Then why not honour your pets as your table names, or have a pet-friendly table plan? You could honour the pets you've ever owned together by naming them on your plan as the names for your tables.

You don't have any pets, but you love animals, and you want to acknowledge that fact at your wedding? Then why not have a charity donation to your favourite animal charity as your wedding favour? Or donate food and blankets to animal shelters. Have an animal theme wedding, safari-themed, butterfly-themed, or dog theme? You get my drift.

Vegan? Then go animal free in all aspects, makeup, hair products, no leather shoes, no silk clothing, and vegan meals, just to name a few things you could do.

Other animals that could be involved in your wedding!

- Falconry, have a bird ring bearer.
- Owls, have an owl ring bearer.
- Doves, hold a dove release to mark your journey together.
- Llamas, go on a llama walk, or have a llama ring bearer.

Whatever your decision, take regard for the safety of the pets, only use reputable animal handlers and make sure they have all the necessary requirements and insurance needed.

**Notes;**

# Children and your wedding

If you decide that you are not inviting all children to your wedding, maybe you only want the immediate family there with their children, or you don't want any children attending at all, stick to your decision, and let your guests know in advance so they know and they can make alternative arrangements as it wouldn't be very fair for you or your guests if they just showed up presuming all were invited, you may get a few disgruntled guests this way.

To not have any children at your wedding may be an easy decision to make if you have no children of your own, you have adult bridesmaids, and none of your immediate family has young children. You could put it on your invitations that it is an adult-only wedding. This way, any guests that have children know in plenty of time and can decide what they want to do.

If you want your favourite niece as your flower girl or your stepson as your page boy, it's clear that children will be invited to your wedding, but do you want to limit the numbers? Maybe only invite immediate families' children? This decision will ultimately depend on your budget; maybe you only want your children there and no one else's, or maybe you can invite all your guest list and their children to save on any arguments. Ultimately you will need to figure it out yourself as usual, at a formal wedding, children's meals are half the price of the adults, be budget conscious and do whatever you feel is best and is true to your budget and yourselves you never know, given the option some guests may choose to not bring their children so they can enjoy themselves and not be parents that day.

To keep children entertained during a wedding, maybe through the speeches, and the bits a child might find boring, you may want to consider these options;

- activity packs on their table setting
- give them a role to do in the ceremony
- mini lego kits at their table setting will keep them busy
- a balloon modelling kit, or even a magician at your wedding, great for adults too
- a wedding bouncy castle on the grounds
- giant games for outside

Make sure a parent is sat next to their child, even if they are your bridesmaid.

Maybe you have a designated child table for the older children as part of your plans.

Don't give the children markers or paint as part of their activity packs; let's not be silly.

Maybe organise a treasure hunt for the children to complete.

Have a games table, with board games, cards, dominoes, that sort of thing.

You don't want them to be on their phones constantly.

Watch them entertain guests by dancing on the dance floor without a care in the world.

**Notes;**

# Bridal dress attire

## History of the wedding attire

It's 1840, and Queen Victoria is getting married to Prince Albert. She wore a white satin dress with flounces of lace, a diamond necklace and earrings and a sapphire brooch.

Traditionally before Queen Victoria, brides would wear their most expensive, best dress to their wedding, and they would be in any colour. Back then, white outfits were only worn by the wealthy as it was only them who could afford white clothing.

The trend of wearing white didn't become a thing until after Queen Victoria. Mostly, it was red outfits.

Veils were introduced by the Ancient Greeks and Romans; they thought a veil would protect brides from evil spirits and also hide their beauty. Presently they can make you feel feminine, sexy, mysterious and very bridal. Veils can have different meanings for different cultures.

Traditionally weddings used to take place in the morning, and grooms traditionally wore their morning attire, hence the meaning of the morning suit. Nowadays, black tie is the norm for formal attire or lightweight suits for informal weddings.

Dressing bridesmaids, similar to the Bride, was traditionally done to ward off evil spirits. In today's times, brides wear white dresses, and bridesmaids wear outfits to flatter themselves and the Bride.

## Wedding dress styles

### A-line

The style that will never go out of fashion. It flatters all figures, as it's fitted across the bust, nips in at the waist to emphasise it, and then flares and flows out wider to the bottom. It draws the eye upwards. Almost any neckline can be used, and the fabric of the dress can come in a variety of forms. It is a very versatile style.

### Ballgown

The fairytale style, this style is the most traditional, classic and royal-like choice for brides with a straight or athletic body shape. Fitted across the bust, having a natural waist, and then a dramatic full skirt, flowing in either pleats or gatherings of your choice material, this gives the illusion of having wider hips. Ball gowns tend to be off the shoulder, either in full or part and expose some or all of your arms too. Layers of tulle or crinolines go into these dresses.

### Empire

This style of dress is a universally flattering style. It has a fitted bodice and then drapes out from under the bustline rather than the waistline. An empire-style dress can typically have a long flowing type skirt, but as trends change, there are new lengths of empire dresses out in bridal shops, bringing the trend to the high street bridalwear shops. Empire dresses can be off-the-shoulder, low cut, with sleeves, or without sleeves; there are lots of variations to this wonderful style of dress.

## Mermaid

A tightly fitted style of dress, going from the bodice to the knee, then flares out below the knee in a dramatic, bold style "tail" effect, like a Mermaid. Elegant and impressive, the tail of the dress is detailed in ruffles, lace, tulle or beading, giving off the right mermaid fin effect. A romantic style of dress, creating an hourglass figure, accentuating all your womanly curves. Great for ladies with an hourglass figure or triangle shape, this type of dress does not hide anything. It is all on show.

## Sheath

Also known as the column shape, this style of dress is best for brides with sleek, slim figures, ideal for women of petite stature, as it will add length to your stature. Fitted to your body and falls straight to the floor, like a slip. Fabrics such as crepe, chiffon or tulle are used as they are light and flowing and work wonderfully with this type of dress. An effortless, sexy, elegant and understated type of dress that will show off your natural figure.

## Square neckline

This type of neckline can create the illusion of a longer neck and can draw attention to your collarbones; it provides a contrast to your curves. Ideal neckline for women with shorter necks, narrow shoulders, curvy hips and large bust areas. This type of neckline is great if you want to show off more shoulders and can be found on dresses with straps or sleeves. A timeless, trendy dress shape.

## Sweetheart neckline

Flattering for all shapes and styles, a look that will never go out of fashion. Its heart-shaped neckline highlights the bust area and collarbone area, which is ideal if you want to enhance those areas or create an illusion of curves. Gives off a long and lean appearance and is very flattering, a classic choice for brides. A very romantic, demure style for brides.

## Strapless

Strapless wedding dresses come in various different types of neckline shapes and are basically dresses with no sleeves or straps. Strapless dresses are great for ladies with a pear shape or a straight shape as this type of dress will create curves and will be visually appealing, usually fitted at the bodice, so the dress stays up and accentuates all the right parts, showcasing your shoulders, back and arms. A beautiful, timeless piece.

## Hints, tips and suggestions:

- Have a look through Pinterest bridal photographs to help inspire you so you can choose ideas for the styles of dresses you like. You will be amazed at seeming to know what you like and don't like in a style of dress. You may surprise yourself.
- Figure out what kind of vibe you are going for, how formal or informal you would like to go, and try to narrow down the styles you like.
- You want to choose a style of dress that flatters your body shape, and if you choose a neckline that will go with your body shape, the look you're going for and the style of your wedding in general,

you are onto a winner. There are many options to choose from; try not to get lost in the dress shop hype, and stay true to yourself.

- Wedding dresses are not the same size as normal high street clothing shops, as they are made in different countries from all over the world, they could be up to two sizes different.

- Depending on what style of dress you go for, this will determine what you need to wear underneath your dress. For instance, you wouldn't wear a visible bra with straps with a strapless wedding dress. There's lots of shapewear and good quality underwear to give you what you need to exude in your dress. Just make sure it fits well, and you are comfortable.

- There are also lots of things that can be done if your dress doesn't quite fit you in the right places. A wedding dress seamstress will be able to guide you with this, but to give you a few ideas, you could add some bra cups to certain areas to fill out the bust area, accessorise with a beautiful sash or wedding belt to cinch you in at the waist or get a panel added to the back of your dress to give more room to breathe.

- Don't be put off by the sizing in bridal shops. If you are a size 14 or above in high street shops, in bridal shops that are classed as a plus size, and as some bridal shops don't stock samples in sizes above a 12, my suggestion would be to phone in advance and see if they are able to get any samples in your size or not, as most designers do offer plus size dresses.

- There are also bridal dressmakers you could go and see. They actually make the dress to fit literally. Your wedding dress would be a definite one-off, then, with no replica anywhere. There are also plus-sized bridal dress shops that specifically only stock dresses from a size 14 upwards. Give them a whirl. Love the skin your in.

- You want to be wedding dress shopping at least 10 months before your wedding, as some dresses will need to be made from scratch and sent over from a different country. Unless you buy off the peg/rail, then you don't need as much time. That is if you don't need it amending either, wedding seamstresses do get booked up quickly, and their work can be time-consuming.

- Once you have your wedding dress in mind, your florist will be able to guide you into the type of bouquet that will go with your wedding dress and emphasise it and complement it correctly.

**Coloured wedding dresses:**

Yes, white or ivory wedding dresses are traditional, and yes, they can make you feel more bridal, but if colour makes you happy and you want to stand out, and do things differently, then you should accommodate this in the way you can.

By considering a coloured wedding dress, you would definitely be breaking the norm, and there are lots of designers that offer black, red or even green wedding dresses.

If you are not wanting to be as bold as that, some designers do their dresses, in soft blush, nude, antique colours, soft golds, and champagne tones. Still different from white and ivory.

A freelance wedding dressmaker can offer whatever colour you want really as long as the material allows it, which may be a safer option if you start to struggle with high-street bridal dress shops.

Choose a colour that suits the style of the wedding theme you're having; colour is a reflection of you and your feelings and how you are perceived. It can also show how it can make others feel.

Weddings don't have to be about wedding themes that are only made up of two complementary colours only. Weddings are adapting, and couples can now have weddings that are as individual as they are themselves.

Dare to be different and make a statement.

Approach your dress shopping experience with joy and anticipation; you might try on one, three or ten gowns, but when you have found "the one," you will know.


**Bridesmaids dresses**

How many bridesmaids are you having? Have you chosen them? This is your first job with regard to bridesmaids.

Then ask yourself;

What season are you getting married in? What theme are you going for? What do you envisage your bridesmaids wearing? Once you have your colour scheme in mind and your overall wedding theme. Your bridesmaid's dresses should fit in nicely once all these other decisions have been made.

Bridesmaids will all have different body shapes and different dress tastes; not only do the dresses need to match these points, but they also need to go with your dress, and they all need to compliment each other too and your wedding.

If your wedding dress is vintage inspired, then this inspiration needs to flow into your bridesmaid's outfits too.

Are you having a whimsical, romantic wedding? Maybe consider your bridesmaids to be dressed in flowing fabrics, ruffles, and that kind of feel.

If you are having a bold and trendy wedding, maybe your bridesmaids would be better in different outfits, with different fabrics, or something fashionable that goes with your trendy theme.

If your wedding dress is a coloured dress, then make sure your bridesmaid's colours complement your coloured dress.

Keep the formalities the same with all your dresses. If you're wearing a floor-length dress, then your bridesmaids will look odd in short dresses. Keep the lengths similar.

Are the bridesmaids contributing to their dress expenses? Be realistic about your wedding budget. Does it stretch to paying for all your bridesmaid's outfits? Or should they contribute to other aspects of their outfit, like their shoes or accessories? Talk to your bridesmaids and see where the lands lie if your budget doesn't stretch.

Your flowers and accessories should flow throughout, too. If your bridesmaid's outfits are in a Cadbury purple colour, they are probably not going to have a lot of those coloured flowers in their bouquet; you don't want colour on colour; you want to emphasise your outfits and make sure everything compliments throughout so it all goes, and your photographs will showcase this too.

Overall, make sure your bridesmaids don't outshine you, the Bride; their dresses don't have to match the exact detailing of your dress, they don't need the same neckline as you have in your dress, they don't need all the bling on their dresses that you have on yours, it's your special day and your spotlight.

## Groomsmen

When considering the groom and his groomsmen and what their dress attire should be, you want to consider the venue, the formalities of the day, the weather and the season you are getting married in, your wedding theme and your colour scheme.

Choose and pick out the bridesmaid's outfits first before shopping for the men because then you will have the colours correct, and you can match things like ties and pocket squares for the men with the bridesmaid's dresses.

If you're getting married in the countryside, you may want to consider a tweed style suit, or if you're in a chic setting with a monochrome feel, a tuxedo may be more fitting. There are many styles of suits for many different themes, so you want to get it right on your wedding day, so it all flows.

Traditionally a groom and his groomsmen wore matching suits, but nowadays, there is no set rule to matching. It is down to personal preference. Maybe the groom can look slightly different with a different coloured tie or shirt to stand out differently from his man? Or maybe you want to be all the same so you all match, and it's all formal. Anything goes, as long as it goes with your idea for your wedding day.

Your budget will decide whether your pay for the groomsman's suits or not. Have a discussion with your men about it, you may want to consider them just hiring their suits out to save on cost if they are funding it themselves, or maybe they can contribute and buy their own shoes for their suit if your budget can stretch to buying their suits for them. Better to know what everyone is doing so plans can be made and put into place.

Don't leave it too late to organise the men, they will still need suit fittings, and just like women, men come in different sizes too, so some suits may need to be adjusted, so plan in advance so the time you will need is on your side in this case. You want to be sorting the men out at least a month before your wedding day.

Don't forget the mens accessories, depending on the suits, you may need cuff links, braces, shoes, and matching socks.

And for their buttonholes, make sure they are not colour on colour, so if their tie is pink, maybe do their buttonhole in the colour of their shirt? White or ivory. If you are having a rustic wedding, maybe the buttonholes can be more countryside inspired rather than a formal buttonholes. Maybe you want to match the bridesmaids and the groomsmen together with their flowers and colours, and the groom matches a flower and colour out of the Bride's bouquet. Genius move on keeping everything flowing and matchy-matchy.

Set the tone, set the colour combinations, set the formality, and remember there is no hard rule that says that all of the men need to match perfectly if you or they don't want to. If the groom wants to be in a patterned jacket whilst all the other groomsmen are in plain block colours, then go with it; the groom may want to stand out just as much as the Bride does. It's got to suit your style and personality as well as the wedding.

**Notes;**

# Wedding Extras

With so many things to think about when planning a wedding, amongst everyday life, work, family and friends, some things may get forgotten, so I have collated a list of bits and bobs that may have to go back on your to-do list, or it could be something you've not even thought about and quite like the idea of doing for your wedding, along with the things you may want to kerb so nothing gets ruined on your day either;

## Kerb it:

- you may want to kerb any arguing with your partner towards the big day, your both stressed, chill, enjoy the build and just go with the flow.
- try not to bicker with family on the run-up to the wedding and on the day itself, in fact.
- you don't want to alienate your friends by talking about your wedding plans nonstop, yes they are interested and yes, they do want to know things, but leave some details to the imagination or the day itself.
- try not to obsess over losing weight. There is no rule that says only size 8 people can get married, and remember the reasons you fell in love and got engaged in the first place; it probably had nothing to do with your weight.
- be careful of overspending. Ideally, you don't want to start your married life in debt.
- try not to take the mickey at work. You may want to do some planning whilst at work, but keep it to your break times.

- you won't be able to control everything on the day. Some things will be out of your hands, decisions may have to be made, and plans may have to change at the last minute, try to remain calm and have people in place to help or advise should something happen.
- don't skip meals, keep hydrated, and be kind to yourselves.
- don't wear heels that are too high for you.
- remember to keep things real. Remember why you're doing this and what it means to you both.

**Remember, remember:**

- Personalised ribbon to tie on your bouquets.
- Memory charm to fix to your bouquet with pictures of loved ones no longer here, so they too can be with you as you walk down the aisle.
- Personalised direction signs for outside your venue.
- Action or Lego figures for your buttonholes for your themed wedding.
- Personalised champagne flutes or wine glasses for the two of you to toast with.
- Gifts for each other for the morning of the wedding.
- Cake knife or sword.
- Guest book or guest signing item.
- Sparklers for those fabulous photographs.
- Children's activity pack.
- Page boy/flower girl sign for walking down the aisle.
- Reserved signs for the bridal party at the top of the aisle.

- Outdoor wedding? Somewhere for guests to put their coats, like a rail.

- Personalised wedding favours.

- Confetti/bubbles.

- Break your shoes in both of you, have plasters to hand in case.

- Handbag with your lipstick, perfume, mints, and touch-up stuff. Keep it at the reception, so it's handy for you for toilet visits.

- Comfy shoes at the reception.

- Accessories for your hair, and your jewellery, don't forget to take your engagement ring off.

- Keepsake box for all your Knick knacks after your wedding.

- Alternative reception setups and ideas, cigar station, whisky bar, gin bar, cocktail bar, toasting marshmallows, making s'mores, chocolate fountains, sweetie cart, beer barrels.

- Caricature pictures as entertainment.

- A bucket list for guests to write down what they think the couple should do within their marriage, suggestions, advice, and things they should go, see or do.

- Take away boxes for cake, desserts, and food leftovers. Guests can take it home.

- Photograph props for funny photography.

- Insurance, wedding, travel, visas if required, honeymoon tickets, passes, foreign exchange, airport travel, pack your bags in advance, passports.

- Buy anything you need for your honeymoon in advance, like clothes, toiletries etc.

- If you need vaccinations for travelling, make sure you have them in time.

- Take any medications you need on your day, don't forget.
- Get all your waxing treatments done in time on the run-up to your wedding.
- Don't fake tan the night before.

Plan for every eventuality and scenario and if you don't do that, get someone on board that does; it can be life-saving sometimes.


**Notes;**

# Hen and Stag do's

Hen and Stag parties have been a wedding tradition since the Ancient Greeks started these celebrations.

Traditionally "hen" means a female bird, which is where the name originates from, the women of your life would gather together to feast and celebrate the up-and-coming nuptials and the marking of womanhood.

"Stag" do's originate from the Ancient Greeks in Sparta, when feasts were held to mark the male becoming a man and to celebrate the end of his youth.

Fast forward to the modern day, and it is now something that couples tend to still do before they get married, celebrating the up-and-coming nuptials and the next stage of their relationship. Couples tend to still celebrate separately, but it is not unheard of for couples to celebrate together jointly. It is totally down to your beliefs, relationship and what you want to achieve.

They may be called different things in different countries, for instance, Americans call them Bachelor/Bachelorette parties, and in Australia, it is called Buck's night. But the concept is still the same. It is an honoured tradition.

Gender-neutral parties are known as sten and fox parties.

**Hen Night**

It is an unwritten rule that your Bridesmaids organise the Hen party, but that is not the case in all circumstances. You may want to take the reigns on the planning yourself, and there is no right or wrong way of doing it.

I would say the first thing you need to do when planning a Hen party is to make sure your Bridesmaids know what it is that you like, what you would prefer to do, what is acceptable and what you do not under any circumstances want to happen. They may think they know you inside and out, but you would be surprised.

Make sure everything is included for the activities you have planned, whether it is dressing up bits, or items needed for the Hen. The last thing you want to happen is a disastrous turn of events, and for it to not be anything about the Bride aka You.

Think about all the people involved and who is to be invited. Everyone will have a different budget, make sure it is cost-effective for all to take part.

Make sure all planning goes to plan, and have a hen night checklist if you need to.

Don't worry and have fun!

**Here are some ideas for Hen parties:**

Cocktail-making parties, Spa days, Dance classes (pole dancing, salsa, burlesque), Meal in a favourite restaurant, Escape rooms, Night away, Afternoon tea, Drinks and a bar crawl, and Heritage site visit. There is so much more for lots of different tastes.

You won't please everyone, as we all like different things, but as long as the Bride is happy, that is great.

## Stag Nights

Usually organised by the best man, and will usually mean the groom will have nothing to do with the planning of it.

But if you are wanting any kind of say in the arrangements, my suggestion would be to have a word with the groomsmen and tell them what kind of thing you are looking for, what you would really like to do, what you are not looking forward to doing.

What you should probably expect from a stag do humiliation and embarrassment of the groom, whether that is by dressing him up, playing party games, or getting him so drunk that he won't remember much. Say goodbye to your Liver for the weekend. Shots anyone?

Here are a few ideas that you could pass on to the groomsmen for stag party preparations.

Beer pong, paintballing, laser tag, clay pigeon shooting, archery, axe throwing, go-kart racing, casino, comedy club, lad's night out in the clubs, medieval banquet night.

Stag parties usually mean more the merrier, with lots of pranks, jokes and banter.

Once-in-a-lifetime party.

**Notes;**

# Honeymoon

Some may say that this was probably the best bit of getting married, the chance to go on a romantic trip with your loved one, a once-in-a-lifetime holiday maybe, giving you a chance to tune out the rest of the world, and start your married life in happy bliss.

It never started out like this, to be fair, as holidaying never really became a thing till the 1800s. Back in the day, a married couple would just spend their first few days and weeks visiting the family that never made it to their wedding, and the word "honeymoon" came around from drinking a honey-infused alcoholic drink called mead after their first "moon" together as a married couple. The mead drink would have been a gift from guests that attended their wedding. It was believed that it held aphrodisiac properties to help with conception. That is how the "honeymoon" tradition and its name came about. A couple's first marital passage.

In today's society, though, what does this mean for a newlywed couple?

Modern-day honeymoons can now come in various ways, what with busy schedules, families and financial constraints being some of the hurdles some couples may face, newlyweds are now sourcing alternatives to the tradition of the "honeymoon". And here are a few suggestions for you to consider as you are about to celebrate the beginnings of married life.

## Mini Moons

Are you stuck for time after the wedding? Finances at the moment mean you have to save up for the main honeymoon trip of a lifetime; maybe you are getting married abroad but would still like to celebrate this wonderful tradition. Whatever your reasons, maybe consider a short trip, a city break, a weekend away in a country lodge, or go for a getaway that doesn't break the bank, and you can still just be together to celebrate your wedding, just the two of you. Your journey into the next stage of your relationship is to be made.

## Family Moons

Do you have children? Cannot get anyone to look after the children whilst you go away together? Then go on a magical family holiday and celebrate all together. How special will that be to be all together, sharing your memories together? There are lots of places you could go, centre Parcs, beach sun holiday, holiday lodges, Disney, as long as you are all together it doesn't matter where you are.

## Buddy-moons

Instead of a trip for two, why not take a trip with friends? Celebrate your marriage with friends and do something with those chosen loved ones that are right up your street, increase your celebrations with friends. Whether it is a full holiday altogether or your friends join you on a certain portion of your trip. Celebrate in a unique way, your way.

## Honeymoon

Whether you are going to have an extraordinary honeymoon together, a romantic trip away together, a historic culture visit, or somewhere where you can switch off, turn off, relax and not worry about anything. The world is your oyster; as long as you have each other and you are in it together, it doesn't matter where you are, but here are some suggestions and top destinations for honeymooners for you anyway.

**Top destinations**

- Paris, one of the most romantic cities in the world.
- Italy, the culture, the history, the beauty and the food.
- The Maldives, the most beautiful beach holiday you can imagine.
- Bali, relax and switch off.
- St Lucia, romance and beaches.
- Mexico, the buzz, the vibe, the fun.
- Florida, Disney's home town and the option of doing a twin centre to encompass your holiday full-on.
- Iceland, the sheer beauty.

Decide together what your choices will be

Where will your honeymoon take you both?

**Notes;**

# Wedding gifts

Nowadays, it's common to send out a gift list to your guests, so they can choose their own gift for you within their own budget.

There are several parts to the wedding gifts scenario. There are the gifts you give out to certain loved ones, bridesmaids and groomsmen to say thanks for all they have done for your wedding in planning and preparations. There are also the gifts you maybe exchange between yourselves the night before your wedding or on the morning of your wedding, a token of your love for each other. And then there is your wedding gift list for guests to buy you a gift for your wedding day.

So, let's break it down,

The bridal party you usually buy gifts for to thank them for their help in the planning and preparation of your wedding are usually;

The Mother of the Bride and groom

The Father of the Bride and groom

Maid of honour, Bridesmaids and flower girls

Best men, page boys and groomsmen

Any family member that has maybe gone above and beyond your expectations, maybe they have baked your cake or made your flower arrangements.

Maybe your wedding planner

Some couples choose sentimental gifts to give out as their thank-you gifts, maybe a special photograph framed with a nice verse attached to it or an item that you can be sure they will love and approve of.

A traditional gift for Mums is usually a bouquet of flowers.

A traditional gift for best men and groomsmen is either a pair of cufflinks or a hip flask filled with their favourite tipple.

I think whatever you choose, they will be appreciative of the fact that you have gone out of your way to get something for them by way of saying thank you.

These gifts are usually given out during the speeches, so you can always say what you think and feel at that time too, a way of expressing yourself in thanking them too. It will mean a lot and be gratifying to you both and to your loved ones.

**Gifts for each other:**

I would say this is probably more of a new trend, buying each other a gift for your wedding day to express your love for each other, maybe writing a love note for your loved one to read on the morning of your wedding, super cute and very meaningful.

Maybe you want to surprise your partner with something engraved on their watch or their wedding ring, either words engraved onto something which means something to you both or even the date of your wedding and time you got/or are getting married.

What about their favourite perfume or aftershave to wear down the aisle?

Something personal, meaningful, sentimental, and evokes your love for each other.

### Gift list:

Asking for wedding gifts may seem almost slightly alien to some, it is a strange concept, but rather than receiving four toasters, two microwaves and a hoard of champagne glasses, having a wedding gift list almost feels like it's a practical thing to do. So how do you ask your guests for presents? Here are a few suggestions;

Put it on your wedding invitation. If you're registering a list at a department store, or you want certain gift cards for a particular store, whatever you do, make sure it's on the invite with how the guest can reserve the gift, that way, they know what they can do and choose something at their own will and within their budget.

If you have a wedding website, put it on there with all the details of how guests can reserve their gifts for you both.

If not doing either of those, then get your family and friends to spread the word about what you're hoping for as a gift.

As some couples already live together now before they get married, a department store gift registry may seem impractical, so if you want something different to household items, may I suggest opening up a gift registry for your honeymoon, like a honeymoon fund registry, where guests can pay donations towards your honeymoon, they can pay for treatment whilst you're on your honeymoon, they can pay for an attraction, or even just pay towards the currency for your honeymoon. A house deposit fund page is a good one, and a home improvement fund page is also a good one too. Great alternatives to the traditional gift registry and may feel more up your street if you're already living together.

Maybe tell your guests how appreciative you are for their gifts, explain what it is you are trying to achieve with their gifts, and make them feel a part

218

of your growth as a couple. They are helping to set you both on your way, in whatever direction that may be.

**Notes;**

# Checklist

What you need to be organising, planning and booking at what stage in advance of your wedding day.

Here is your handy checklist, to do list;

**10 - 12 months to go:**

- 
- Work out your budget, prioritise and work out where you could save or spend
- Work on your wedding ideas, themes and colour schemes
- Work out a rough guest list for a rough idea of numbers
- Choose your bridal party, bridesmaids, groomsmen
- Go venue shopping, choose where your ceremony and reception are going to be, reserve your date
- Take out wedding Insurance if you want it
- Create your wedding website if you are doing one
- Send out your save the dates if you're doing them
- Hire a wedding planner if you're not doing it yourself
- Start researching and seeking a photographer, videographer, caterers if required, and a celebrant if required; if happy, reserve them
- Get inspired with wedding outfits
- Attend any wedding fairs and wedding shows, be inspired
- If you're having a destination wedding, research it, book it

## 6 - 9 months to go:

- Research and book any more suppliers required for your wedding. This includes DJs, entertainment, wedding cars and transportation

- Make arrangements and decisions with your florist and get them booked in

- Go cake tasting and choose your cake designer

- If you're going with a stationery supplier or not, discuss and go through the style of your stationery requirements and the wording you want for it all

- If you've decided to have a gift registry get this organised so it can go on your invitations

- Update your wedding website in accordance with the arrangements made

- Where are your guests staying for the night of your wedding? Do hotel arrangements need to be made, if so get them arranged

- Go shopping for your bridal party's outfits, bridesmaids, groomsmen, flower girls, page boys, etc

- Organise your guest list for your hen and stag parties. Go over any details needed for this with the person organising it if it's not you

- Organise menu tasting for your venue, choose your menu

- Start thinking about your honeymoon and what arrangements you need to sort, get prices together

**3 - 5 months to go:**

If you haven't got the mens suits organised yet, get these sorted and booked in

- Get your wedding favours sorted
- If your wedding involves being outdoor, or your needing table linens or any other party rentals, reserve any of this now
- If you need any childcare, pet care, or any children's entertainment, get these booked in
- Do you have any rehearsal dinners or wedding rehearsals? Get these booked and organised with the people who need to attend
- Organise anything that you are doing as a surprise for your partner, whether that's a cake or something else
- Finalise your guest list, get your addresses correct for posting invites
- Finalise your stationery wording, get your invitations sent out and finalise any other stationery items you require
- Write up your wedding vows if your writing your own
- Finalise your ceremony readings if you have them
- Confirm your menu, drinks package and any other catering requirements
- Write out a timeline of your day, or get your planner too. Make sure all the details are correct and everything is in order

- Go for any makeup and hair trials. If you're happy, get them booked in
- If you want to start a beauty or fitness regime for your wedding, start this now
- Go ring shopping, order any engraving that needs doing to them
- Finalise your honeymoon plans, check your passports, and get any other documents together that you may need for it

**6 - 8 weeks to go:**

- Sort out how you're going to store your rsvp notifications and your guest's menu choices, and any dietary requirements
- Do you have a plan b in place if your outdoor wedding doesn't go to plan? Maybe think about having one
- Confirm your details with your suppliers
- Do you need a marriage license, divorce papers, or any form of name change paperwork? Get all this in place and applied for if required
- Start your dress fittings if required for any amendments to your outfit
- Get your accessories in place and ordered, and get your lingerie and any undergarments bought or ordered for your fittings
- Planning on a dance performance for your first dance, if so book the lessons and start practising
- Start breaking in your wedding shoes
- Maybe give the hen and stag organisers a nudge to see if everything is in order and planned

- If you have received any early wedding gifts, maybe get a thank you card written out and sent
- Get any children's activity packs together and ordered, along with any welcoming things you're doing for your guests

**3 - 5 weeks to go:**

- If your holding a rehearsal dinner or have arranged anything else rehearsal-wise, make sure your invites have gone out
- Finalise your wedding vows, your readings
- If you're having a pre-wedding photoshoot, get this done and organise what photographs you want with your photographer
- Finalise your details with your videographer
- Sort out your music list for your wedding, either on your own devices for your wedding venue or your DJ, band or any musicians
- Sort out who is doing speeches, organise the order and start writing your speech if required
- Where are you staying the night before your wedding and the night of your wedding? Get this sorted if it's not with your venue
- Collect your rings, check the engraving for spelling mistakes
- Do you have your something old, new, borrowed, blue in order
- Get together your guest signing arrangement, unity candle, your toast glasses, and anything extra like that bought
- Buy your wedding gifts for whoever you're buying them for

- Go for your final dress fittings with all your accessories so you can see the final picture
- Chase up any rsvp people
- Do your table plan and seating arrangements
- Pay your final bills

## 1 - 2 weeks to go:

- Give your venue, caterers, stationery and any other supplier that may need to know your final headcount
- Collect suits
- Finalise all your details with all your suppliers
- Confirm arrival times for all suppliers
- Pack an emergency kit for every eventuality
- If the weather is looking bad for your outdoor wedding, maybe discuss your plan b and put that in motion if at risk
- Pack for your honeymoon if you are going after your wedding
- Book in for any facials, hair treatments, waxing or other treatments now
- If you have artificial flower arrangements, make sure they are delivered in advance of your wedding
- Go on your Hen or stag do
- Make sure any of your DIY bits are completed and packed

**3 days to go:**

- Get your manicure and pedicure done
- Pack your accessories up for anything needed for the wedding
- Meet up with your bridal party, make sure all is ok
- Stay away from any drama or family issue
- Attend your rehearsal dinner or any other rehearsal item on the agenda
- Make sure all your bridal party know what they are doing, and organise the men to take their suits back if they are hiring them out
- If you're paying any suppliers on the day, make sure all this is prepared for
- Assign a bridesmaid for gift collection at the wedding, make sure it goes somewhere safe
- Attend any church rehearsals

**Day before:**

- Collect dresses and outfits for wedding
- Any arrangements you have done yourself, make sure these are at the venue, if someone else is putting them out make sure they know what and where. If you haven't got anyone to do it for you, make sure all is done before your wedding
- Get to the place where you're staying the night before
- Make sure you've got everything you need, any documentation, money, vows, speeches
- Make sure you've got your day after your wedding clothes packed and gone with you

- Make sure the best man/woman has the rings
- Have an early night, get your beauty sleep

**The big day:**

- Give yourself plenty of time to get ready
- Make sure you eat breakfast, you will need it to keep you going, and you will need the energy, eat something that won't bloat you
- Stay hydrated

**Wedding advice and tips**

- Make sure you greet everyone at your wedding, do the rounds
- Take a few minutes for yourselves; it can feel overwhelming. Take a deep breath
- Appreciate your efforts, take it all in
- Don't exercise too hard and cause yourself a mischief
- If you're not looking to have a skin breakout or be bloated on your wedding day, on the week of your wedding, if you avoid these foods and drinks, it will help you feel your best on your wedding day;
- carbonated beverages
- salty foods
- caffeine
- processed foods
- artificial sweeteners and sugar

- dairy

- spicy foods

- cruciferous vegetables

- beans

- Try to drink as much water as you can on the run-up to your wedding. Your skin will thank you and reward you

- Get as much rest as you can on the run-up to your wedding, as you will be exhausted


**After the wedding/honeymoon**

- write your thank you cards out if you're not having them printed

- send your thank you cards out

- complete your gift registry if you've done one, and exchange any unwanted or duplicated gifts

- have your dress dry cleaned

- keep in touch with your photographer and videographer for your pictures, DVDs, albums


**Notes;**

# What you cannot control

You've hired all your suppliers, and they are there to make your life easier. Trust that they can do this, trust that they are going to do their part in your big day, and don't stress about the little things.

Ask your suppliers if you've missed anything. If you are unsure about anything or worried about anything, just ask; obviously not on the day of your wedding; a bit too late to do that then.

Don't stress about the weather; it's the one thing you are not in control of at all; the only thing you can do is be prepared, umbrellas, patio heaters, fire pits, blankets, parasols, air conditioning, fans, you get my drift. Have a plan b at your venue if possible.

If it rains on your wedding day, this is a sign of good luck. It signifies your marriage will last. A knot that gets wet is very hard to unravel, so as you "tie the knot" on your rainy wedding day, it means your marriage will be just as hard to unravel. Embrace it. Stay positive.

Rainbows will make a beautiful backdrop for your photographs. Remember that if the weather has been thunderous on the run-up to your big day.

You can't control the pollen count, but obviously, you can prepare yourself and watch the weather on the run-up to your wedding and take control and reduce your chances of having an allergic reaction to a high pollen count or the bright sunshine, take extra precautions if you're going abroad for your wedding. Take your allergy meds.

Unforeseen circumstances can appear at the last minute without pre-warning, things like a sickness with guests etc.. it can't be helped, and it will be something you'll have to get your bridal party to deal with on the day. It may mean extra food for others, don't take on the challenge yourself of sorting this out. Leave it for your bridesmaids and groomsmen; you've got enough to contend with, don't add it onto yourself.

## The finale

Take it all in, embrace yourself in the little things, and try not to overlook anything. If there's one thing I know about weddings, it is that the day goes by very quickly. Take in as much as you can, as it will be over in a flash, and get your guests to take photographs so you can see your wedding through their eyes. All the candid shots will make it fun, seeing your wedding through the eye of a loved one. It's going to be magical, you are marrying your soul mate, your best friend, the love of your life, and at the end of the day, that's all that matters.

Thank you so much for buying my book, I hope you find it very useful, and I hope you've made lots of notes and journaled your way through it. And even if this book is a gift for a loved one that is planning their wedding, may I take this opportunity to wish you all the best. Enjoy planning your wedding. I would love to hear how you have got on and if anyone would like any more help or guidance. Please find me on Facebook and Instagram.

Kate Harvey Bridal Mentor

With the sincerest love, warm wishes and hope for your future.

Kate

# About the Author

Hi there I am Kate,

I have been in the wedding industry for the last 15 years, but I have a floristry background going back over 25 years and I began my wedding journey as a wedding florist in a local one stop wedding shop. This is where I started my journey with my own business. I have been very fortunate to be able to share couples most special day of their lives and it's been a privilege to have done so over the years. My creations have donned castles, stately homes, hotels, registry offices and have traveled far and wide to countries like Cyprus, South Africa and America. I have truly loved with a passion what I have achieved and have loved every minute of being a creative link in the wedding chain, I truly have felt blessed. And to be able to help and guide couples in their planning journey through the stages of wedding planning is a dream come true. I am very grateful.

Let me know how you get on!

Much love

Kate x